Advice to Young People

Advice to Young People

Daisaku Ikeda

translated by Robert Epp

WORLD TRIBUNE PRESS • *Los Angeles*

International Standard Book Number: 0-915678-07-1
Library of Congress Catalog Card Number: 76-469
World Tribune Press, Los Angeles, CA 90406

Printed in the United States of America

Contents

Preface

I am quite fond of talking with you young people.

Each time I meet one of you so brimming with hope, each time I talk with one of you and see your sparkling eyes, I feel a fresh sense of amazement at the way each of you seems charged with limitless potential for the future, with a personality characteristic only of the young.

Nor do I know a greater joy than seeing you steadily mature. I sincerely hope that you young people of Japan — no, I mean of the entire world — will retain that luster of hope in your eyes and fashion a future of peace and happiness.

This is the hope that fills me when, on various occasions, I have the opportunity to speak with you. I have also received countless questions from you which touch on all sorts of problems: school and study, parents and friends, and even views of man and social affairs.

Some of these questions have been extremely difficult to answer because I am not a specialist in the area you asked about. But I have been amazed again and again to be showered with such astute questions — questions which penetrate to the heart of the problem.

Specialist or not, however, I have tried my best to respond to each inquiry with all the sincerity I could muster.

This book is a collection of responses to certain questions received over the past several years, mostly from junior high students. I have expanded my answers slightly so as to make sense to young people in general and not merely to the one who asked the question.

I value and honor each of you as an upstanding individual personality, the same as I would any adult. When I deal with you young people, I consider you ladies and gentlemen, believing this the most appropriate attitude to take; nor do I intend to treat you any differently in the future.

Of course, although tender in age, you are in no way different from adults with regard to your worth as human beings. In the same way that men and women are fundamentally equal, that no occupation is to be especially honored or despised, and that no distinctions should be made in terms of one's social rank, there is certainly no justification for differences in degree of respect just because of a person's age.

Needless to say there are areas in which one cannot say that young people and adults are absolutely on equal footing. From the viewpoint of social roles and the inequality of responsibility, for example, children cannot always demand the same rights as adults. But such distinctions (based as they are on the fact that adults are seniors and young people are juniors on the road of life) do not really amount to fundamental differences between young and old.

This conviction and this attitude motivate me both to assume that you young people are fellow human beings and to answer your questions with that assumption foremost in mind.

Beyond that, I trust that you will accept what I have written merely as advice from one who has walked a bit farther down life's road.

After all, I have neither any outstanding mental gifts nor an especially remarkable background. Quite an ordinary, commoner type, the son of a dealer in edible seaweed, my youthful heart harbored the usual concerns and, like everyone else in those days, I fled the ravages of war.

But human society is composed mainly of just such ordinary people. That is why I think youngsters need the advice of someone who has simply had more experience than they. They do not need sermons delivered with the air of one dispensing wisdom, as though he were a sage or a man of special virtue. Geniuses and people with unique abilities are a small minority; the vast majority of us are plain, ordinary people. In fact, come to think of it, it could be that just such a common person might be best equipped to counsel the young.

What I would like to stress here is not only that this line of thought runs through all the advice in the pages that follow, but that I intend throughout to set great value on human life, above all paying due respect to the personality of each individual.

When we look at the problems of life, whether major issues like war and pollution or minor ones like trivial spats between people, we find that they arise from the same basic source: a contempt and lack of respect for fellow man.

In order to construct an ideal society it is necessary to

improve its framework. Regardless of how splendid a framework we make, however, society itself will not in the least be improved until each and every individual shows respect for human life. Only when people concentrate on accumulating the wisdom that sets great store on life itself, only when they agree that the highest value is respect for human beings, will the structure of society match the ideal. Only then might society become the sort of place where each individual enjoys peace and prosperity. Creating such a society is the task you young people will face in the future. It is at this time, however, *now* during your youth when you are building the foundation on which your entire life will be built, that I would like you to make this basic viewpoint part and parcel of the very way you live and breathe.

If you examine the qualities that make a person truly human, you will discover that they derive from a viewpoint that respects life and the individual. This is true whether you speak of courage, of a sense of justice, of sincerity or consideration for others. Consequently, you might say that when this basic pattern of thought has been firmly established in a person, his character development will be complete in terms of his being *truly* human.

I am not confident that the advice given in this book will, with respect to concrete details, fully satisfy youngsters who wonder about such problems. I can say at the very least, however, that I have tried to illustrate in my responses to you this standard of respect for life and for each individual.

Let me close with the sincere hope that each of you might mature into a positive-thinking, resolute and vigorous young adult with the ability to assume responsibility for the future of Japan and the world.

July 25, 1972 — Daisaku Ikeda

Advice to Young People

On Study

QUESTION:

People say it's important to study hard in junior high. But it seems to me that our studies amount only to preparing for tests.

ANSWER:

Why study? It is possible to offer a number of reasons. In a word, I think we study so we can develop into complete persons, into whole human beings. What we learn of the Japanese and English languages, for instance, can be put to direct use in social life. Even such subjects as mathematics, which may not seem to have a direct connection with life, are important for nurturing logical thinking.

That is why you are not studying merely to pass exams. And that, too, is why I agree that one must never study *just* to pass a test.

Sad to say, however, the state of affairs at this moment appears headed in the direction you indicate: there is a strong tendency to study merely to pass tests. To get a job at a good company in Japan, one must go to a first-class university. To get into such a university, one must attend a first-rate high school. To enter such a high school, one must score well on tests in junior high. Nobody can deny that it seems students study exclusively to pass exams. Because this is clearly a defect in our present educational system, and in society as well, the system must be reformed.

Nevertheless, it is wrong to refuse to study just because society is bad or just because the educational system is bad. It is your business to change society. You will obviously have to study hard now and provide yourself with the capability to do that.

This also relates to problems other than study. Just to say you are against society because it is bad is mere negative criticism. It's only an excuse to escape responsibility. Isn't it more characteristic of young people who have set their eyes on the future to consider what must be done now in order to improve society? And then to carry it out faithfully?

If you give it some thought, you will realize that since human beings are lazy, most study only because there is a quiz — the test is their inducement to work. By no means do I intend to give across-the-board approval to the test system. But if there were no exams, most people would probably not study very much. Many would find it delightful if there were no tests, although this situation doubtlessly would provide cause for serious regrets in the future. In the end, even if you imagine that you are studying only to take tests, the tests actually do have some benefit.

I would like to suggest that you change your attitude toward tests. It is not a matter of studying *for* tests. I mean, you should not consider tests as *the reason* you study. Think rather of tests as the stimulus for study, or as steps on the way to mastery. So if your study makes headway as you prepare for exams, it seems all right to study hard for them.

One often reads in stories dealing with sports about a coach's severe discipline, and how, even though the athlete was driven to work hard initially by the fear of being "bawled out," when he matured and looked back on the experience he was grateful for the coach's strict discipline. In the same way, even if tests seem the objective, they can be the occasion both for increasing your scholastic attainments as you hurdle them one at a time, and also for great personal growth.

QUESTION:

I try to do my homework, but our house is small and I don't even have a room to study in. And since I have a number of brothers, it's noisy, too, so I can't settle down and concentrate on my books. What can I do?

ANSWER:

I suspect there are many youngsters plagued by this very problem. After all, there are not likely too many in Japan who can settle down and study leisurely in their own rooms. In one way or another, most junior high students probably suffer from the same experience.

But then study is a battle with yourself. Even if a person has his own splendid study, possesses all the reference works he wants and has a first-rate tutor, none of it will amount to much unless the all-important individual involved applies himself earnestly to his books.

Certainly it may be easy to study when your environment is perfect. But environment is only one factor contributing to effective study. It is nothing more than that. If we ask ourselves whether those blessed with ideal conditions for doing their homework actually devote themselves wholeheartedly to their studies, and if we ask whether the grades of such students are all that good, we must answer: Certainly not! Among your acquaintances is probably someone who puts up with poor conditions for study and yet makes top grades. In the long run, how much a person is willing to study is a matter of his *will* to study; it depends on how he grapples with the problem of studying in an imperfect environment.

If you really have the desire to *study hard*, you can do it under any conditions. There is a famous anecdote about the time Thomas Edison (1847-1931), the "king of inventors," studied while he worked on a train as a teenager. But you need not be an Edison. Anyone who burns with the desire to study will not be stopped by unfavorable conditions.

You've probably had the experience of being so absorbed in a magazine or television program that you were not aware your mother had called you. There are times, I imagine, when you become so engrossed that you didn't even hear the siren of a fire truck. It's the same with study. When you sit down at your desk determined to study in dead earnest, you will be less aware of the clamor around you. That is why it seems to me that the basis of the problem is firming up your own attitude toward study.

Beyond that, the next most important matter is ingenuity. The smaller your house, the more necessary for you to find ways to study with the utmost efficiency in the face of your handicaps.

One method, for example, is to utilize the local library or the school library. You might also talk over the problem at home and, after setting aside certain hours when the television will be on, arrange your studies when the set is not in use. Moreover, in the event that things are so noisy you cannot get anything done in the daytime, you might try studying at night.

In any case, it seems to me that it is rather beneficial for your future development to be forced during these growing years to study amidst difficulties which you imagine are just too much to bear. To put it somewhat bluntly, I think you should recognize such an environment as a blessing in disguise.

The future will confront you with many difficulties. There will be storms and gloomy nights. It will be rather rare, I suspect, that you'll be able to work under conditions you would regard as favorable. At such times, what sort of person do you imagine is capable of overcoming all obstacles with the greatest self-assurance? Is it the person who spent the critical years of his personality formation in a comfortable environment, or the one who blazed his own path through trials and tribulations?

You may definitely think your prospects for success very grim at the moment. You may be thinking, "Oh, if only I could settle down and study in silence!" But the mere experience of overcoming unfavorable conditions will create a secure basis for future accomplishments. I would hope that you become a stalwart young man who not only refrains from bemoaning poor conditions, but also uses them as the basis for personal growth.

QUESTION:
My grades are terrible so I'm really worried. How can I get good grades?

ANSWER:
Not being a school teacher, I can offer only certain fundamentals. Be sure to see your teachers for concrete details.

Practically everyone from primary school through college wants an answer to your question. But it seems to me that there is no particular mystery about getting good grades. In my opinion, to start from the conclusion, you cannot do it short of putting your nose to the grindstone and plugging away with tireless zeal.

Some may protest that they have been given fewer brains than others. I don't think, however, that raw intellectual ability differs that much from person to person. My own teacher, Josei Toda (1900-1958), was an educator who claimed that although we always talk of "sharp" people or "dull" people, there is actually only a hair's difference between them. The Scottish philosopher Sir William Hamilton (1788-1856) said, "Genius is simply the result of hard work." The French naturalist Georges Buffon (1707-88) said, "Genius is nothing more than the maximum exercise of perseverance." Both statements illustrate what I mean.

So then success is largely a matter of endeavor. Consider for a moment a professional baseball player. No matter how excellent a hitter he might be, he can't maintain a decent batting average without regular practice. If you ask what this practice consists of, it's merely dedication to swinging the bat. This means that by constant repetition of that simple, that totally fundamental, act of swinging the bat, a person develops into a first-rate hitter. It's the same with a pitcher. One can become a star only by the constant daily repetition of something anybody can do: throw a ball.

I believe that success in study is achieved in the same way. One sits down at a desk, reads the text, takes notes — there's not much variation; in fact, one might even call it uninteresting. What do you suppose would happen to the hitter, however, who tires of practicing his swing because he finds it boring? Or to the pitcher who becomes indifferent to pitching practice? Regardless of the batter or pitching star involved, lack of practice would soon show up in below-par performance.

Thus, in order to get good grades you must "practice" too. What is vital is ordinary diligence, *period.* That means doing your class preparations and reviewing regularly and properly. That means listening earnestly during class to what your teachers tell you. It is perhaps no exaggeration to claim that your grades will be determined by this sort of diligence. The conclusive factor is whether you can persevere in maintaining this attitude to the end of the course.

Next are study methods. What reference works should you use? How should you take notes? Such questions depend largely on individual differences so they cannot be answered categorically. But I can suggest that there is no substitute for discovering — on your own through trial and error — the method most appropriate to your own personality. There are probably good ways and bad ways to go about it, but even if you let yourself be instructed in the beginning by friends or others, don't you think it would be best in the end to come up with a method that fits *you* to a "T"?

My own observation is that many of those who make poor grades seem to lack a solid foundation in the basics. That's why I believe it might be a good idea for you to dedicate yourself to a program of persistent review, concentrating on your textbooks. That would include even books you are not studying at the moment — I mean, go all the way back to your first-year texts and read them over carefully. If you do, you'll certainly discover things you ought to have mastered but which you didn't fully understand. If you can find what was not clear to you, you'll be on your way to successfully firming up your foundation, because if later on you can ask your teachers for the answers or get friends to tell you, you'll end up mastering the material.

In any event, never lose heart but plug away systematically and steadily and your grades will improve.

QUESTION:

They say that it's important to study when one is a junior high student, but I also hear that it's important to participate in extracurricular activities. Yet if I do a good job in one of them the other suffers.

ANSWER:

My conclusion is that it may be rough but you really ought to be involved both in study and in some extracurricular activity. Let me explain why I think this is true.

During your junior high school days you lay the foundations of your entire life. If you were going to build a building and began with a flimsy foundation, later on you would be unable to make that structure as high as you'd like. I mean you can erect a tall building only after you have laid a deep and firm foundation. It's the same with life. If you do not discipline yourself now for the days ahead, I can say that it will be nearly impossible to grow up to be a person of some stature.

Laying the foundations for that sort of future is, to put it bluntly, wholly a matter of disciplining both mind and body. Training the mind means to absorb knowledge; training the body means to build a healthy physique. One might also say that the mind is the "cultivator" of a number of areas, including harmonious relations with friends, perseverance, and the sort of general knowledge you need to become a full-fledged member of society. That is to say, the mind's ability to integrate these areas helps to lay the foundation for your entire life. That is the basis upon which all your future professional knowledge and skills will rest and, thus, the basis on which your accomplishments as a member of society will be viewed.

To achieve these ends, it is vital not only that you study

but that you participate in extracurricular activities as well. Some of your fellow students, driven perhaps by the excessively success-oriented "educational mother" type, may do nothing but study. And yet no matter how splendid one's academic record, good grades alone do not amount to growth as a human being.

And so, during these important junior high school days, don't you think it necessary to try getting involved in everything you can — with the spirit that you'd like to try to test the limits of your abilities? It would definitely be too much to become *completely* involved in both studies and extracurricular activities. As you say, I think that if you become overly involved in the one there will be times when you might neglect the other. I would like to suggest, however, that it might be unnecessary to fear that this would have an undesirable result.

True, we have the proverb, "He that hunts two hares at once will catch neither." But I suspect that you may rather end up confining your abilities too narrowly if — in these youthful days that reach towards the future — you exercise an excessive amount of caution. Go ahead and make some mistakes! Even errors will, you can rest assured, become assets for building your future. My hope for you is that whatever two hares you pursue, you might go about it with all the youthful determination you can muster.

There may be times when you will probably suffer the agonies of frustration. But do not think for a moment that you can't endure the pain, for suffering and agonizing over life's dilemmas is truly vital to your growth as a human being.

In the very act of trying to solve your dilemma, you'll discover the means to go on, the source of strength you need, and maturity as well. No human being grows unless he suffers, unless he *works* at growing. Only wheat which has been tamped down under the farmer's foot can survive the winter and mature, awaiting spring's sunshine to ripen. This means that when young people struggle through anxieties and ordeals, you lay a firm foundation for the future.

At this point I would like to offer two further pieces of advice concerning how you might become involved in both studies and extracurricular activities.

The first is the fact that being involved in these two areas does not mean that you will always be exerting the same amount of effort in both arenas. There is always the danger that by devoting yourself evenly between the two you'll do an equally inadequate job in either. You will have to invest all your energies in studies when you have exams, when you must prepare an important subject, when you have to review; at other times, when you are vigorously involved in extracurricular activities, you ought to spend more time on them. The main point is that it is vital not to mismanage the balance between the two areas.

The second piece of advice is the fact that it is important for you to concentrate one hundred percent of your energy on other activities when it is time for them. This is true of everything you do. There is no reason to expect desirable results if you do not concentrate wholeheartedly on whatever you are engaged in at the moment.

Most to be avoided is filling your head with extracurricular activities and such things when you should be studying. Or to think about your studies when you should be involved in other activities. And yet a surprisingly large number of people do not concentrate solely on what they are doing at the moment. It may not be an exaggeration to say that nearly all who fail to operate skillfully in both areas are people who cannot concentrate on doing one thing at a time.

At this moment your problem is to decide between studies or outside activities. But as you develop into adulthood you will find that you have to make decisions about involvement in any number of different activities, not just two. Beyond that, should you wish some day to make a contribution to society, you'll have to learn to do a good job on many different tasks. In order to be prepared for such a time, I'd like you to begin right now trying to develop the habit of devoting all your energies to one thing at a time.

QUESTION:

I'm often told it's important to read, but aren't textbooks enough? Why should I read a lot of different books?

ANSWER:

If your only concern is to improve your grades, it may be all right to read only those books related to your classes. In the future, however, if you are to become a broad-minded person with a wealth of human qualities, I think it important to read all sorts of books — intensely and extensively — from the time you are young.

Reading enables you, first of all, to absorb the experiences and knowledge of others by becoming involved in what they have written; acquiring a storehouse like that will come in handy. Secondly, you not only acquire knowledge, but books enable you also to discover what is new to you, so you will be able to broaden your thinking. Ability to take a broad perspective is extremely important in life.

Thirdly, familiarity with the characters who appear in novels and stories will stimulate your innate sense of justice and your natural creativity. Before you know it, you'll find you have an expanded awareness of what it means to live as a human being, and you will also discover what you should do with your future.

You may get some instruction along these lines at school. Rather than being merely taught about them, however, you'll find later on, when you have some perspective, that if you have read and grappled with these problems on your own you are likely to get a lot more out of the experience.

There are quite a few people now active in society who were so moved by books in their youth that they became oblivious to the passage of time. The stimulation from what they read in those days determined the direction they later took in life. Nevertheless, even if books do not have quite that effect, there are numerous examples of people whose creativity and sense of justice — cultivated through reading when they were young — continue to influence their personalities long after they became adults.

During my youth I was one of those sickly kids who liked books better than anything. I used to go to second-hand book shops to rummage around for all sorts of novels and legends to read.

One book I read during those days has left an indelible impression on me: *Les Misērables*, a novel by the Frenchman Victor Hugo (1802-85). Of course I was too young to understand Hugo's profound philosophical ideas, but I was deeply moved by this beautiful story of love. Jean Valjean, released after having served nineteen years in prison for stealing a loaf of bread, eventually comes to love the orphaned Cosette as his own daughter. In the face of the persecution and criticism of neighbors and associates, Valjean brings her up to be a fine young woman.

This book made such an impression on me that, when I had finished it, I thought to myself that someday I'd like to write a similar long novel — one which, like Hugo's, would involve people in the "crucible of excitement."

Then, later on in my teens, works like the poetry of Walt Whitman (1819-92) and the *Divine Comedy* of Dante (1265-1321), both of which I read avidly, exerted a powerful influence on the development of my character. Various circumstances prevented me from obtaining a satisfactory college education, but I now feel quite confident that I was able to enrich my adolescent years by reading books.

One can polish the pearls in his mind by reading books! Those which you might tackle may include a number so difficult that you feel you'd like to give up before you finish.

But wouldn't the tingling excitement of finishing a substantial book compare with the exhilaration of the mountain climber who has conquered a peak?

Let me quote a famous statement the priest Yoshida Kenko (1283-1350) made in his *Essays in Idleness* (Section 13): "There is nothing more pleasant than spreading a book out under a candle and making friends with people from unknown worlds." Through books we can make friends with people from far-off lands, with people from the distant past.

If you do not wish to become a painfully narrow person, like one who fits into a predictable mold, I believe it important to read many books and, as far as possible, to keep on perfecting yourself.

QUESTION:

I understand it's important to read books and I'd like to do so, but I'm mixed up and not sure which to choose. What sort of books should one read in junior high? Also, which books will improve me the most?

ANSWER:

It is impossible to be dogmatic about telling anyone which books he should read. Much depends, you see, on likes and dislikes and on a person's interests.

As a starter, if you want merely to "get acquainted" with books, it's probably easiest to read about something that interests you. If, for example, you happen to like geography or history, or if you're not good at either but feel like getting control of them, you might start from something relatively easy to read that relates to geography or history.

In the case of history, how about biographies of famous people? In our own history, for example, there are fascinating books about military leaders like Toyotomi Hideyoshi (1536-98) or the stalwart samurai teacher, Yoshida Shoin (1830-59).

If, on the other hand, you are interested in science, there are also easy-to-read books on that topic written for young people; if your interests lean that way you can find many splendid things to read in science fiction. And if you're interested in biology, there are many comparatively easy-to-read books around, such as descriptions of the life cycles of insects or pictorial encyclopedias — assuming you'll begin with material that will add to your knowledge of areas in which you feel an immediate interest.

Such books will, almost without exception, be available in your school library or at your local library, so I imagine that you can visit whichever you please and pick from the shelves (they have been classified according to topics) those

which seem most appealing to you.

If you go about it this way, you'll become more and more interested in reading. And I suspect your scope will extend itself as your interests broaden and you find yourself saying, "Gee, I think I'll read this one, and I'd like to tackle that one too!"

Now then, let me respond to your question about which books you should read in junior high. One way to find out is to make a list of (a) books your teachers or schoolmates suggest and (b) works recommended by magazines written for junior high students. I would imagine that books your teachers suggest, as well as those recommended by magazines and the like, would be necessary reading for you at this time, so they are likely worth checking out.

If I might add my own opinion here, let me suggest that you not limit yourself to works touching your immediate interests. If possible, I'd like to see you read books which will enrich your sense of justice and your sensitivity to the world and to others. For example, I have in mind biographical tales of people who have left their imprint on history, or the masterpieces of world literature.

Particularly after you finish school and go out into the world to make a living will you find that you simply have no leisure for reading literary works. That is why, if you do not read these masterpieces during your junior high and high school days, chances are you may completely miss the opportunity to read them.

The reason I urge you so strongly to read literature is by no means because it was my favorite at your age. But great works of literature invariably contain glistening pearls of wisdom which confront us with human reality. How should men conduct themselves? How can one be truly human? Concerns like these are certainly not limited to people interested in literature.

Even those who like science and math and figure they'd like to become engineers in the future will, I am sure, find that literary works deal with problems that every human being must soberly consider. Although literature may not directly relate to science, there is no doubt that it can influence the personality development of future scientists.

QUESTION:

Even when I set out to read a book, I get bored in a minute. Maybe I'm the kind that can't stick to things. Especially if I start on something like a novel, I always give up halfway through. I just can't seem to get involved in books. What's the secret to learning how to read without getting bored?

ANSWER:

Books are something people find it a chore to get involved in, even when one is lying open in front of them. It's terribly difficult to get going on a book unless you are anxious to find out how the tale turns out in the next installment, or unless the volume opens on page one with a particularly gripping story.

Writers who publish books are also aware of this problem. Even with a coherent plot in mind, an author will agonize quite a bit over how to manage his opening paragraphs. One world-class literary giant is reported to have said that he spends just about as much time contemplating how to write the first few lines of a book as he does turning out the several hundred pages that follow.

Switching back to the reader's standpoint, you can see how difficult it is to get started reading. From the outset, books are simply not easy to become involved in. Although you complain that you quickly tire of a book, I certainly do not think you should imagine that this is the way things must be.

As to your question, "What's the secret to learning how to read without getting bored?" let me say this: why not begin by reading a book on a topic that interests you?

You say you get particularly bored reading novels. What that means to me is that you are not yet in the mood to read such works. Go ahead and read something that deals with a topic you are concerned about, something you think you'd like to look into. Those are the kinds of books you should read — even if you do get slightly bored part way through. Something like comic books, for instance, can be read quickly. For the most you'll be able to finish them before you know it. But you must start at some point to know what it feels like to finish reading a book.

Beyond that, make up your mind to plow steadily through works you know you must read, even if you dislike doing so — textbooks, for example.

Thus, to begin with, it's a matter of finding and reading those books which interest you or which you feel you want to read. Even if you think the task difficult, or even if you should find the book hard to understand, never mind, go ahead and finish reading it.

Whenever you manage somehow to read a whole volume, you'll gain a sense of fulfillment from having completed it. And out of that satisfaction will come the desire to read still another book. Little by little as this happens you will grow fond of books and, sooner or later, find yourself reading them through to the end, even if it costs you some effort.

The point is that you must first of all complete *one* book on a topic that interests you. Your success in finishing will give you a sense of satisfaction and a taste of the joy of reading. No matter how you approach the problem, however, you will not be able to stick to your plan unless you do experience such a sense of fulfillment and joy.

It's very much the same in sports, too. When you first put on a baseball mitt and had a ball thrown your way, you were probably at a loss as to how to catch it. But if you left it at that, you could never, never experience the joy of playing baseball. Only by continuous efforts, only by being a butterfingers again and again, only by being forced each time you miss to go running after the ball, will you gradually learn how to catch it. Eventually you'll be able to do it expertly. At that point you can develop a zest for playing baseball.

As long as you keep them at a distance, however, printed words are especially difficult to become "chummy" with. On the other hand, words in print have the characteristic that their "foreignness" disappears when you get used to dealing with them. Then they become surprisingly good friends.

Consequently, when people tackle books on subjects related to their interests and get used to dealing with the printed word, they usually learn to finish reading even those works which they had previously considered hard to become interested in. But of course you have to make some effort to develop to that point. I would like you to take it as a challenge to do so and, by all means, I hope you will not accept your present attitude as the last word.

QUESTION:

Mother always scolds me whenever I read comic books or detective stories, but I think they're all right to read now and then for diversion. What do you think, are they bad for me?

ANSWER:

I do not think it is good for you to read *only* comic books, but as you say if only for diversion, I do not imagine it can do much harm. For one thing, you may become the sort of rigid person without a sense of humor if you never read things like comics when you're young.

Of course there are good and there are bad comic books. Particularly among the most recent selections do we find some that are unwholesome. The publication of such comics is certainly not a desirable trend and creates a problem we must devote some thought to.

The existence of this undesirable trend should not mean, however, that all comic books are bad. Comic books are filled with superb humor and novel ideas; it is possible to absorb such humor and wit naturally as one moves along from frame to frame.

Wit and humor can become extremely helpful, serving as a breath of fresh air throughout your life, particularly in a society where people tend to be quite formal with each other. Furthermore, one might say that humor cultivates the kind of appealing personality liked by everyone: the cheerful, positive sort of person who faces every hardship with a smile.

This is why I think you cannot ignore comic books as a means of cultivating a more expansive sensitivity and visionary conceptions. Some say that adults in our society display quite differing sensibilities depending on which comic books they read in their youth.

When I was a boy I read such comics as "Dankichi's Adventures" and "Blackie the Stray." Memories of frames from those strips even now flow vividly into my mind, frames which at that time encouraged me to dream of the future or caused me to chuckle.

Let me turn now to the problem of detective stories. I think it is quite all right to regard them in precisely the same light as comic books. I understand clearly the reasons your mother worries that you are reading detective stories. Their plots, after all, are bound to deal with such anti-social themes as murder and crime, and so she is probably concerned that — should you read piles of such stories — you might be adversely influenced by them. Particularly do the criminals who appear in "whodunit" stories work out quite intricate schemes, more often than not outfoxing the detectives and investigators who try to track them down. So it is understandable that readers become absorbed or at least interested in plans for the perfect crime.

So then, from the viewpoint of a mother who desires the wholesome growth of her child, it is logical for her to think it best for you to be as little influenced by such material as possible.

One cannot say, however, that everyone who reads detective stories becomes a criminal. In fact, such stories have nothing whatsoever to do with the reasons most felons become involved in crime. That is why I find no objection at all to your reading detective stories should you wish to. These stories do concentrate heavily on the psychology of the criminal or on his ingenious schemes for committing some crime, but the process of deduction in investigating the clues is also a vital aspect of these novels.

Whenever we approach problems that need to be solved, we cannot possibly discount the important deductive skills portrayed in mystery stories: thinking logically in a step-by-step manner about the facts of the case, the clues, and always beginning with what is "given." This is the fundamental approach, the basic method to deal with any facts in a coherent manner.

Detective stories can consequently help a good deal, both to make your own thinking more precise and to discipline your mind to flexibility, making you open to more possibilities.

QUESTION:

I have a friend who always takes notes on books he reads. He never fails to jot down the title, the way the author looks at things, and his own impressions of the book. Do you think, generally, that this is how one should approach books? I'd also like to know whether you think it is better to read a few books slowly or many books quickly.

ANSWER:

After you have finished reading a book, it is certainly effective to write down what you learned from it, how it moved you, as well as any passages which impressed you, and the like.

The reason is that merely by writing these things down you can make better sense of the book's contents. Thus you will be able to get a much firmer grasp of what the book is about. Accumulating such notebooks on your reading will, moreover, be a private source of joy; it will as well strengthen your sense of being enriched by your reading. And as time passes, when you look over notes on the books you've read, you'll be able to see how you've grown and what you were thinking about when you were a lad.

That is why, if you can keep such notes, it will be beneficial. Taking notes on every book you read will, I suppose, take a good deal of time, but then you need not write a lot about every book. It is perhaps sufficient to list merely the author's intentions in writing the book, the book's main theme, as well as noting in abbreviated form your own impressions of the work. You will find that even notes as brief as these will increase your ability to deal with books.

There is no need, moreover, for you to take notes on all the books you have read. After all, you have doubtlessly read works which did not particularly impress you or which were not very interesting. That is why it's best to limit your note taking to books which moved you or which you found extremely instructive. The concrete form the notes will take is up to each individual, for there are as many methods as there are note takers, so just take them in any way you please.

Now we turn to your second question, should reading be intensive or extensive? Of course nobody can make a categorical judgment as to which is better. Much depends, among other things, on the nature of the individual and the content of the book.

But this is not simply a matter of deciding to read broadly. It depends on the book itself; there are works which should be read time and again. This is particularly true, for example, of books which have deeply impressed you and which you may even have felt like rereading. The reason for going back over a book with profound content is that, as you reread it, you can thoroughly master it by discovering new concepts — ideas you were not aware of — and by gaining a clearer understanding of those parts you could not fully comprehend the previous time you read the book.

In the West there is the proverbial expression, "Fear the man who has mastered a book!" This means that nobody is superior to the person who has total control of a single volume, for such knowledge confers the ability to influence one's society and his age.

For literary people, and for many others as well, I understand that the "single volume" to be mastered in the West has been the Bible, Homer's *Iliad* or *Odyssey*, or in economics, Adam Smith's *The Wealth of Nations* (1776). I am certain that such a book, one which may have been read many times, has exerted a lifelong influence on those who have left their marks on history.

Viewed in this way, it is extremely important to dig deeply into a single book. Needless to say, the expression, "Fear the man who has mastered a book!" does not in the least mean that you should read and study only *one* book. If you read only a single work and neglect all others, you can become the sort of person who is quite narrow and biased.

But you will probably have to read many, many books in order to discover the one which you would like to study for a lifetime. As you read extensively, savoring all sorts of books, your own concerns and the direction of your life will gradually become clear to you, and you will find yourself anxious to study intensively a few among the many books you have become acquainted with in your extensive reading.

This is why the question of whether to read intensively or extensively is perhaps most appropriately resolved by suggesting that the two approaches actually complement each other. One reads extensively to broaden his point of view; one reads intensively to deepen his comprehension of a book's content.

On Future

QUESTION:

I think I'd like to go into government when I grow up, but the moment I see a terrific movie I feel like becoming a film director. Or when I read a book, all of a sudden I want to be a scholar. I'm confused. Is it normal to have such mixed-up ambitions?

ANSWER:

During youth, one's curiosity is stronger than at any time in his entire life. Moreover, it is natural that those with a receptive mind immediately respond to the challenge of new goals and aspire to achieve them. At your age, it would be odd indeed if you lacked such dreams and aspirations.

That is why, although you feel you want to go into government, when you see a movie you think you'd like to become the sort of person who can put together such a splendid film. Or when you read a book which was particularly instructive, you feel the urge to become a scholar. This is not strange at all. It is rather important for you at this stage in your life to have various opportunities to take in all manner of experiences, to absorb them and to keep alive your many dreams and hopes for the future.

Beyond that, tasting and absorbing a wide range of experiences will deepen and enrich your desire to work in government. I say that because at your age there is no special course of study to prepare you for such work.

Rather than special courses, however, you should see how fundamental it is for a person in government to have a broad view of things and to be a warm human being. The English economist Alfred Marshall (1842-1924) said that a warm heart and a fine brain are absolutely necessary in leaders. This apt expression seems a fitting description of the human qualities required of a person going into government service.

Most current political leaders do not appear to have such qualities; they do not seem to be warm human beings. That, in a nutshell, is why we do not really have a government which relates to and considers the welfare of the people. If you feel strongly about going into politics, it is vital that you take advantage of the terrific receptivity and open-mindedness of your youth so that you can actively absorb art and movies and literary selections that focus on the reality of man's life, thus developing your personality and perspective.

There is something else you might keep in mind. We talk of the dreams of our youth and the future of young people, but the aspirations of youth by no means determine one's future. Rather is it true that our youthful hopes frequently end up taking a completely different direction. In most cases, the confusing dreams we had when we were children ultimately focus on a single thing as an individual matures.

Speaking from my own experience, I must say that what I am doing now is in no way related to what I dreamed of doing when I was your age. My present existence is something I could not possibly have imagined when I was in junior high.

This is not to conclude, however, that it is meaningless to have dreams and hopes. Although I never could have guessed I'd be doing what I am now, the yearnings and hopes I embraced as a lad are definitely being realized in my present position. My personal motto, my main desire in life, remains the same: I want to be the sort of person who, no matter how many years have passed, persistently maintains and reflects in his whole being a passion that stems from inner genuineness.

One's youth is the time of hope. A particularly wholesome picture of youthfulness is to have so many dreams for the future that one is at a loss to determine what he wants to be.

Consequently, I think there is definitely no need for you to feel anxious about the future on that score. I think you should push ahead and study a variety of things with the attitude that it is truly a joy to have dreams that are expansive. And I would like to see you continue cultivating those wholesome youthful aspirations even after you become an adult.

QUESTION:

I want to be a professional baseball player, but Dad is a dentist and he wants me to take over his practice. What should I do?

ANSWER:

Problems dealing with one's future vocation are always somewhat difficult. But at the present stage, since you are still in junior high school, don't you think you have plenty of time before making a decision?

There are several reasons why I think so. Your current desire to become a professional baseball player may change in the future. On the other hand, even though you now want to play pro ball when you grow up, it is possible that you may lose confidence in your physical strength, discover limits to your ability, or — even should you be assured of your skills — you might well feel that you're not good enough to play with the pros. These are all possibilities that could happen along the way.

Moreover, if your ability and talent to succeed as a professional baseball player are recognized, it is quite possible that your father will change his mind about insisting that you become a dentist. From his viewpoint, perhaps he opposes your desire because he is unsure to what extent you actually possess the capability and makings of a pro ball player.

They say that the main ambition of boys in elementary school and junior high is to play pro baseball. Among my own acquaintances, as well, I often hear that their children want to play professional ball.

Any red-blooded boy who sees a pro execute a fine play, who sees him smash a home run to turn the game around and win the applause of the hundreds of thousands of fans in the ball park or watching on television, will most naturally feel that he'd like to do the same.

That is precisely why your father may lightly regard your desire to play pro ball. He could be thinking it is the same passing ambition seen so frequently in average boys your age. And that, too, is why you should at this time go on enjoying baseball and playing lots of it without worrying your head about the future.

Sports are something you cannot afford to miss; they build a healthy mind and a healthy body. I feel strongly about that, for ever since youth I have been sickly. Obviously it is vital that you study hard when you are young, but it is equally vital that you build up a body capable of working to its full capacity in whatever situation you find yourself in the future.

No matter how outstanding your school record, good grades will not do you much good if you have a weak constitution and have to take to bed frequently. Moreover, when you see everything in total perspective, it does not really make a great deal of difference whether or not you have a terribly sharp mind. Much rather does it seem that quite a number of people have ruined their careers because of frail health. Perhaps it is not too much to claim that, in real life, the basis of success is a healthy body.

Now, for a lad as young as you, though you adore the sport it does not seem all that vital to decide *now* that your entire future will be baseball playing. I suspect that as you mature your hopes and desires will also grow in quality and depth. And during those years you will doubtlessly discover a vocation to pursue.

I cannot tell whether it will be baseball or dentistry. If, however, it turns out that you do not think your vocation is to take over your father's dental practice, you'll have to talk in detail about your future with your entire family, including your dad. Let's leave any specific answer to your present question until then.

QUESTION:

I have no idea what I'd be qualified to do in the future. I often hear about how everyone has his own "talents," but how do I go about discovering mine?

ANSWER:

It is not easy to ascertain what one is qualified to be. Some, aware from childhood of their vocation in life, display particular abilities in that direction. But such people seem the exceptions.

Generally speaking, most apparently choose their vocations much later than that. They do it when they decide to go on to high school or college, or when they are out of school wondering where they can get a job. Even then, however, one cannot positively state that he has clearly discovered his aptitude for a specific job. Often there are times when the decision is made with the vague feeling that "I seem more or less cut out for this."

That is why we find so many people having become successful in fields actually quite different from those they majored in during college or high school days. I personally know of several who worked primarily in the sciences after junior high and yet have made names for themselves as poets or critics.

Why do such things happen? To answer that, of course, touches on the problem of how one can possibly discover his own talents. In any event, although each and every person has specific characteristics and talents and a specific individuality, aptitudes are something he cannot discover by himself. When confronted with a suitable occasion, however, there are times when a person can suddenly become aware of his talents. For example, because one's favorite teacher taught a subject in which he had always done poorly in an extremely interesting manner, this student may naturally become interested in the subject he used to find a bore. There are many such cases where, in the end, the person involved came around to thinking he'd like to work in an area he formerly disliked.

There are, furthermore, probably instances where a suitable stimulus has been provided by a book or a discussion with a friend rather than by a teacher. Through such stimuli, students sometimes discover dormant talents and are able to decide on a vocation.

Obviously you have not yet reached that stage. But there is no reason to be apprehensive just because you do not yet know either what you are qualified to do or what direction your life should take. After all, you are still only in junior high. I think it more important at this time that you study at school and absorb all the information and practical experience you can.

What you learn in junior high is particularly important. It gives you the basic skills you need to be adequately informed as a member of society, even if you go out into the world with no more education than that. If you thoroughly master those fundamental skills, they say you'll have capabilities far superior to a person who studied only half-heartedly — even though he gets a college degree.

Although it is hard to discern one's own aptitudes, surely everyone is interested in or concerned about something or another. While one cannot necessarily claim that his talents or aptitudes lie in such interests and concerns, nevertheless it is true that in many cases some aspect of these interests may lead one directly to discover his vocation in life.

Consequently, along with your school work you should constantly take the initiative in order to come to terms with and master some problem which interests you and about which you are curious. And you should have some *one* thing about which you can say, "I can do this better than anyone."

You need that kind of pride when you are in your teens. It gives you toughness. Even if your job or profession ends up outside your interests, if you have that kind of pride you can make a go of it in real life. And besides, if you have something you can do well, people will respect you and regard you as a useful person in society.

QUESTION:

In the future I'd like to contribute to world peace through music, my favorite field. But when I get to thinking seriously about what it takes to bring peace to the world, it seems that a career in government would be the best and most direct way. How can I resolve this point?

ANSWER:

Certainly it is not only statesmen who prevent wars and bring peace to the world. What is vital is that people from every single walk of life maintain world peace both by transcending differences in occupation and viewpoint and, shoulder to shoulder, by bucking the trends and forces that would generate war. Doubtlessly, peace and war are problems on which government exerts a direct influence. There are also instances where it is impossible to avert the threat of war unless the government steps in.

It is the people, however, who ultimately determine the policies their government adopts. Ideally, each and every citizen keeps a strict vigil over the orientation and direction of his government because each citizen has certain convictions and is aware of his duty to keep his nation from going to war. Thus it is absolutely untrue that you cannot make a contribution to world peace unless you go into government. You can render adequate service to peace even through the music you are so fond of.

Much rather should I say that cultural activities like music provide the basis on which we can actually create a peaceful society. In other words, while it may be the task of statesmen to create the international and social conditions that lead to peace, it is culture which creates the *content* of the peace itself.

I am using the word "culture" in a special way. By culture I mean those activities which give the inner man,

his mind and his spirit, a sense of fulfillment. This is an area into which government authority cannot trespass, an area with which government authority must absolutely not interfere. Through music, the performing arts, poetry, fiction, and the like, the essential nature of culture is to give people hope, a sense of fulfillment in life, and a feeling of happiness.

Among the various cultural forms, music has the broadest appeal and most warms the cockles of the human heart. When people hear a piece by Chopin, they think wistfully back to the days of their youth; when they enjoy Beethoven's "Fifth Symphony," they feel the courage of a phoenix and are overcome with the desire to challenge tomorrow. Music is a precious universal language through which human beings can communicate their feelings over national borders, race and ideology.

Consequently, if you become a fine musician, and through your music communicate the joy of living to the people of the world, that in itself will make a tremendous contribution to peace. One might even say that such a contribution is far more fundamental, far more universal, than what a statesman might accomplish in his efforts for peace.

One reason that war is the greatest of evils is that it nullifies the effects of such splendid cultural activities as music. War and culture are absolutely opposed to each other. Of course, there is a phenomenon called "the culture of war." But for the most such a "culture" only inspires people with the martial spirit or irresponsibly trains them in belligerence. There is practically no exception to the truth that vibrant cultural activities cease under wartime conditions.

Or, to look at it from the opposite angle, what I am saying is this: Freely creative activities and any expansion of dynamic cultural activity not only give the people a sense of fulfillment in their lives; they create a bastion from which man's spirit can oppose war itself. In opposing war, cultural activities help thwart the force most likely to destroy them. Through culture people can, as it were, supervise the tendencies of government and society so that they lead toward peace.

It is with this in mind that I personally would like to see you become a great musician. If those who come into contact with your music are awed afresh by what a precious possession peace is, by the sanctity of human life, and if that awe then becomes the stimulus for increasing the trend to oppose war, you will have made a huge contribution to world peace.

Family Problems

QUESTION:

For some reason or another I no longer find it easy to talk to my folks. I always used to tell them about everything, but now I resent having them ask me about school and what I'm doing.

ANSWER:

My parents have frequently told me that when I was in grade school I reported every single thing that happened, but when I went to junior high I didn't tell them anything. When a boy gets to that age, apparently he tends more and more to avoid talking with his folks.

This is because even a chick, raised gently under parental wings, develops a spirit of self-reliance and seeks to be independent from parental protection when the time is ripe to leave the nest. You are presently at that stage yourself. So in your desire to develop self-reliance, you have begun to find those comfortable wings constraining and even talking with your parents a bother.

Your change in attitude indicates neither that there is something wrong with you, nor that your parents are somehow responsible for the way you feel. You might call this an expected development in the process of growing up, or one of those ordeals you go through to shed adolescence on the way to adulthood.

More than anything, however, the junior high period is an unsettled time of emotional and physical growth. Young people your age have unlimited potential for the future. If such potential develops along undesirable lines, it is possible to make blunders from which it is terribly difficult to recover. At this stage in your development, therefore, it is extremely hazardous to make decisions entirely on your own or to act merely on the basis of personal ideas. But, then, who is most willing to give you advice? Who is most concerned about you and loves you the most? Obviously, your parents. That is why, even though you want to stand on your own two feet, you cannot break with or blindly isolate yourself from them.

I can understand how, in your mind, when you hear the word *parent* you think at once of someone who nags, someone who is nosey. If you don't want to talk about something with your folks, there is no reason why you should force yourself to do so. But if you honestly take stock of yourself, I'll bet you might find a positive personal value in deciding to ask their advice about all sorts of things.

Aside from that, you might look at the situation from their viewpoint. I also have a boy like you in junior high. My fondness for him is constant, no matter what sort of a boy he is, simply because he's my son. Perhaps you will not be able to make sense of this attitude until you get married and have children of your own, but I am sure your parents feel the same way about you.

I do not think you incapable of considering the way your parents feel. Merely to demand independence and freedom with no regard for others is to act like a pampered infant. If you wish to assert your rights, you will — as a mature person — obviously give consideration to others.

If you can get into that frame of mind, I think you will see how quite self-centered it is to have the attitude that since *you* don't want to talk, you need not answer no matter what you are asked. But to set up occasions for dialogue and to talk about school and your friends, even if you prefer *not* to, is to recognize your parents as people. And when you do that, you will for the first time be able to insist that you, too, be respected as a person.

QUESTION:

They say that we junior high students are going through a rebellious stage. I know Mom has warned me that I've been getting sassier lately. But I personally don't think I'm being particularly rebellious so much as I figure I'm right. Do you think I ought to obey everything my parents say?

ANSWER:

This is a delicate issue. I shall try to offer what I think are important criteria to guide your thinking, but you must apply them to your own specific problems.

From time to time one finds mothers and fathers who actually do think that a child must obey everything they say. That's a terribly wrong-headed viewpoint. Even though children are children, they are persons, the same as their parents. Moreover, by the time a child gets to junior high age he has already developed considerable ability to make judgments about issues; he is quite aware of whether it is good or bad for parents to press their own opinions one-sidedly.

This is a question that is of more concern to your parents than to you. Put briefly, it is that I think one should not obey simply because the opinion is presented by an adult.

The criterion for deciding whether an opinion should be heeded has nothing to do with *whose* opinion it is. What is important is the substance of the opinion. If it is sound, it should be heeded carefully even if offered by someone inferior in status. And should it be unsound, then even if it came from someone superior in status the proper response is to hold openly to your own views.

When a person insists on voicing his own opinions, however, the rule of human relationships is that he at the same time pay due respect to the opinions of others. I have already discussed this in dealing with problems of friendship. The problem then boils down to this: Although you say you do not think you're being rebellious because you are right, your conviction of rightness dare not stem from egotism or self-indulgence. Salving your conscience with the notion that you are asserting your freedom to express yourself is to mistake the issues involved. When you do that, you end up with sassiness.

Aside from these considerations, another problem presents itself when your parents are involved. What I mean is that your mother and father are your elders. They have had far more experience in life than you. For one thing, they've gone through the very same stage you are at now. For another, they know some things about life that you do not yet know. And most important of all, who knows the most about you, who thinks most about your future, if not your folks?

Certainly the words of those adults most concerned about you should be worth heeding. From the viewpoint of a teen-ager going through the rebellious stage, there may be times when you'll find their advice old-fashioned, or when you think they are trying to foist their opinions on you. And there may be occasions when you feel that they are merely asserting their parental authority. But if you regard their advice as coming from someone much more experienced in life than you, someone most concerned about what happens to you, don't you think it necessary to give due thought to what they say without rejecting it out of hand?

You may already have heard the famous story about Toju Nakae (1608-48), the "Saint of Omi." Once when he was thirty years of age he returned home during a religious pilgrimage. Conscious of how his mother's hands and feet got so chapped during the bitter cold that she was unable to work in the kitchen, Toju obtained some salve and, undaunted, trudged back home over more than two hundred miles of snowy roads. When he arrived he found his mother drawing water from the well.

"Mother, I'm sure your chapped hands hurt. Let me draw the water."

His mother was surprised to see him. She almost broke into tears on noting the salve her son wanted to hand her. But she abruptly assumed a harsh tone and chided him:

"Didn't you vow that you would not return till you could stand on your own two feet? Yet you've come back home before fulfilling your vow — isn't that a weak-kneed thing to do? I don't need the salve, either. Now you just turn around and get back to your pilgrimage."

When he heard his mother utter these astonishing words, Toju silently put the salve down by the gate, turned around and without setting foot inside the house retraced his steps.

Whether this story is true or false is beside the point. Is it not true that a child often opposes his mother with the thought, "She doesn't know what's on my mind"? From the viewpoint of logic, we certainly cannot say that Toju's behavior was improper. Rather do his mother's words seem unreasonable. If we consider the fact, however, that his mother's response contributed to Toju's growth as a person, we can conclude not only that the mother was wise but that Toju himself was wise in obeying her and going back to devote himself to his search for enlightenment.

We do not live in the early Edo period but in modern times. Perhaps this is no more than a moralistic yarn tinged with the values of an age gone by. And yet there is one thing in this story I'd like you to understand. Even if Toju could not at that moment see the reasonableness of his mother's response, later on when he thought it over he probably said, "Indeed, she was right!"

Rebelliousness can also indicate that one is still acting like a spoiled child. Might we not say that the reason a child can say whatever he pleases is because he *is* spoiled? You might give careful thought to your feelings in this area too.

QUESTION:

It seems that when Dad drinks, his personality changes. Usually he's a very good father, but when I see him like that I just can't respect him. Am I wrong to feel like this about him?

ANSWER:

If I might say so, the relationship between parents and children is mysterious. Although born without wishing to be born, the fact is that a child exists; there is nothing he can do about it. You may not have wanted to be born to your present parents, but there is no way you can undo the fact that they are your parents. These problems are definitely riddles to me. I suspect most people would like to have them unravelled.

What I would like to point out here, however, is the fact that you are your parents' child. I say such an obvious thing because it implies a truth of extremely vital significance.

I mean that as long as your parents are persons, they are living human beings. And nothing is more precious than human life. Even the law punishes a murderer with the severest penalty. Of course, respect for life is far more profound than what is written in the law. No matter how hard one tries, there is no way to express that respect in mere words. A philosopher I deeply esteem takes the view that not even all the treasures of the entire universe are worth the life of a single human being. I cannot help believing this with all my heart.

It is my desire, moreover, that all young people would adopt the same belief. In order to establish stable and permanent peace in the world, I would like you to place an absolute value on human life. Only with the noble spirit of respect for life as your basic principle will you go on protecting it.

You, too, are the steward of a precious life: your own. It is not that you could will to be born, but thanks to your parents you have received life in this world.

With that in mind, I suppose it is obvious what sort of attitude I feel you should take toward your folks. They are your parents, but the mere fact that they are flesh and blood means they have their faults. Rather might one say that, if you probe a bit, you will find them honeycombed with shortcomings. Despite their faults, however, I'd like to point out that, if you recall that they gave you life, you will naturally feel grateful to them and respect them *just as they are*.

With regard to your father's drinking, I wonder whether you couldn't regard his habit more kindly and think of it as a small pleasure? The real world is very stern. It does not allow one to relax for a moment. Your father works day after day in that sort of stern environment, his nerves frayed from morning till night. And all his efforts are expended for the family, for raising his children.

The only place your father can escape the pressure is among his family. He works all day and drags himself home, weary and tense. Would you begrudge him a small pleasure under those conditions? To be denied even that tiny joy is, I think, tantamount to turning him into the family robot.

Certainly there are those who apparently become different people when they drink. But then, liquor has always had that effect so you should not be shocked. Certainly there is no reason to despise your father when he is sober just because you don't like him when he gets drunk. The effects of alcohol will wear off, anyhow, so you might try being glad that he feels happy at the moment.

But if he is the sort who tends to get violent when he is drunk, you might catch him when he is sober and in a good mood and ask him, with the utmost constraint, whether he couldn't drink a little less. If your everyday behavior as his child is commendable, I am sure he will listen to your request.

QUESTION:

I don't have a father so Mother has brought me up on her own. People say that somebody with only one parent often becomes narrow, or that when he goes out into society people will discriminate against him. Does that sort of thing really happen?

ANSWER:

It is extremely regrettable, but in real life you will suffer discrimination on any number of occasions. The preconceived notion that children raised by one parent will be emotionally unbalanced or inferior remains deeply entrenched in our society. It must be said, for example, that if two candidates competing for a job are otherwise equal in ability and the like, most firms would hire the one who has both parents.

But of course it is absolutely untrue that a person is inferior simply because he has only one parent. A prejudice like that has absolutely no basis whatsoever. I know many boys who have lost one or both of their folks. It would be hard to count the number of such young people who are nevertheless positive, wholesome individuals with academic ability, boys expected to have a promising future. Conversely, I know for a fact of numerous young men who, despite having both parents, developed twisted personalities and became inferior human beings. Statistics indicate a startling truth. The families of a surprisingly large number of juvenile delinquents have both parents living at home; they are middle class families which are, to a degree, comfortably off in an economic sense.

What do you suppose this statistic tells us?

The family certainly plays a vital role in the process of personality formation. Nobody can deny how easy it is to end up with character defects, even if a child enjoys a comfortable family life. But the fullness and warmth of the home environment that nurtures the child is definitely determined neither by whether a child has both parents nor by the family's economic situation.

Having both folks and being well-off are important factors, but they by no means determine everything. It is rather the character of the parent which makes the greatest impact on the child. True, the child may have but one parent and the family may be poor, but if that parent is a splendid human being the child, too, will grow up to be a splendid person.

When I saw your question I was overwhelmed by the desire to show my respect to your mother for the tremendous hardships she has endured to raise you all on her own. No doubt she has showered you with tender love. I hope that you feel boundless pride in having such a mother, and that you'll grow up into a positive-thinking, vigorous young man.

It makes me sad to think of the inconsistencies in a society that allows people with groundless feelings of prejudice to have their way. Everyone should be treated equally. How ardently I wish that we might evolve an ideal society absolutely free of prejudice!

As one step along the way to that ideal, I personally trust that you might mature into the superior sort of individual who can demonstrate in his character how absolutely groundless it is to imagine that having only one parent is a handicap. When you yourself become the kind of young man capable of making valuable contributions to society, I think that prejudice, at least in those around you, will melt away.

QUESTION:

Our house is always in an uproar because my folks are constantly fighting. It's a loveless place now and sometimes I just hate being there . . .

ANSWER:

First of all, you ought to realize that truly ideal families are surprisingly few, despite how they might look to an outsider. The famous French philosopher Montaigne (1533-92) says in one of his works that it is more difficult to keep peace in the family than to control the kingdom. Indeed, creating a harmonious family may seem easy but it is difficult.

That is why I think it a mistake for you to imagine that no family is as loveless and divided as yours. Much less is there reason for you to consider running away. Even if you were to run away from home now, you are not likely to find a place where you could be happy. Happiness, when all is said and done, is definitely something you have to fashion yourself in your present environment. That is the discovery made by Tyltyl and Mytyl, the woodcutter's children in Maeterlinck's play, *The Bluebird* (1909).

Now isn't it true that you're thinking it is entirely your parent's responsibility that your home is loveless? If so, that is a terribly mistaken attitude. Certainly your family began with your folk's marriage, and the two of them have worked together to make it what it is today. But since you are already in junior high school, you should be aware that you yourself are now a bona-fide member of the family, equally responsible with your parents for creating a harmonious atmosphere in your home. I should be quick to add, of course, that you do not have the same responsibility in this as they do.

Somehow it seems you have the rather firm notion that

your mother and father are supposed to do it all by themselves. But that is incorrect. I wonder whether you ought not look at this problem from a different angle, from the attitude that — even if you are not entirely up to the task — you should make every effort to get your family back on an even keel, that you should personally try to bring warmth back into your home.

As I have said before, I believe that the person of each child is every bit as precious as the person of each parent. This means that just because one is a child she is not thereby an outsider in the family; rather does she have an appropriate role to play in it.

Well, what should you do about your situation? Primarily you must be a positive and cheerful young lady, a model junior high student. While it is true that human beings are influenced by their environment, it is equally true that they exert an influence on their surroundings by their appearance and behavior. At this time it would not do much good to tell your parents what's on your mind because parents simply do not listen to their children's opinions. But if you are always cheerful and vibrant, I am sure they will as a matter of course become aware that something about you is different.

Let me share with you a husband and wife story I recently heard. Since they had to go to a lot of trouble caring for their grandfather, who found it hard to get around on his own, they constantly maltreated him, serving him his meals, for example, in a crude little box instead of using dishes. But one day they noticed that their own darling little boy had gathered up some pieces of wood and was using them to make something. They asked him what he was making. "I'm building a box," he answered, "and when I grow up I'll have Mommy and Daddy eat from it." His response could not help but shock his parents. They turned pale. After that experience I understand that this couple treated the crippled grandfather more compassionately.

Even if in real life things are not this bad, I suspect that many similar cases do exist. The point here is the effect the little boy had on his parents. It certainly is not true that just because he was a child he was absolutely unable to affect the situation in his home.

In any event, it is your own attitude that is vital. Anybody will agree that it is easy for a person to mature vigorously in a favorable environment. In such a situation, however, the result is often a pampered child, artificially protected like a hothouse plant. By contrast, the person who grows up in an unfavorable environment which he or she overcomes will develop a truly strong character by virtue of the difficulties encountered. An individual's real attractiveness as a human being, moreover, is naturally cultivated in the midst of struggle.

QUESTION:

My family is poor, so I just can't invite my friends over. I feel ashamed about what we have in the house, etc. I know it's not right to have such feelings, but somehow I feel inadequate about a number of things.

ANSWER:

Are you familiar with the following story?

Once long ago the poorest man in the village visited a millionaire and asked, "Sir, they say you own marvelous treasures. Would you be kind enough to show them to me?"

For some time the millionaire had felt the urge to show off his wealth, so he rejoiced at being asked to do so. Pleased as a peacock, he opened his seven storehouses one after the other and showed the poor man his rare treasures.

But the man failed to indicate the slightest amazement as he perused each of them. He only said calmly, "They are indeed splendid, yet at home I have far more precious treasures!"

When the millionaire heard these words he felt sure that this shabby creature could not possibly have anything of the sort. But he could not bear being showed up and, figuring he would go over and embarrass the man, he agreed to stop by at the earliest opportunity.

When the day arrived, the millionaire went over to the poor man's home. He was greeted by a smiling face, crumbling walls and floors laid with frayed straw mats — for, after all, this was the poorest man in town. The millionaire could not imagine that human beings lived in such a hovel.

The rich man no sooner had concluded in his mind that he was right about this fellow's lack of treasures than, with a clap of his hands, the poor man called in his seven sons. They lined up and greeted the millionaire. Facing his sons, the poor fellow said with great pride, "These are my treasures. The value of your treasures can be counted; the value of mine cannot, for there is no limit to what contributions these treasures might make to society. My joy in them increases daily."

Now I doubt that your family is as poor as that of the man in this story. But I will venture to say that your dad's feelings resemble those of this father. What is most vital for a parent is not property or status or honor. Nothing is as precious and as dear as one's own children. Certainly the most meaningful thing in a person's life is to see his child develop into an adult.

Thinking along these lines, you can see how ridiculous it is to feel inferior simply because you are poor. I felt quite disappointed in your attitude when I first read your question because it makes no difference how poor a family is, does it, as long as it has a marvelous possession like you — one which cannot be exchanged for money. And your maturation is, in the true sense, your family's source of wealth.

Poverty! I am no stranger to it, having been very poor in my youth. My father's business failed and, because all four of my elder brothers were taken off to the battlefield, I couldn't go on to high school. I had to go to work. When I was in grade school, my family was involved in the edible seaweed business; I remember having to get up before dawn in the dead of winter to go down to the beach and help gather seaweed.

Even during those trying days, however, I never once thought I was miserable. And now, looking back, I believe it a good thing that I was poor. The mere fact that I have had such experiences helps me understand the feelings of those who suffer from poverty.

They say everyone should suffer a little, even if it's the

sort of suffering you bring on yourself, for suffering builds truly strong character.

Look at your situation this way: your family's poverty is meant to contribute to your future, so grit your teeth and hold on, refusing to let your present sufferings get you down.

Man and Society

QUESTION:

The universe is vast and infinite, and man by comparison is such a small creature. What is the meaning of man's existence in this huge universe?

ANSWER:

When I was about your age I, too, looked at the blinking of brilliant stars in the night skies. My thoughts also turned to the eternal, to the magnificent universe. And I similarly felt that man's life was but a flash in comparison to the macrocosm. But since those were the days when militarism was at its height and when I had to think of going to war, I could not help asking myself about the meaning of man and life.

Among living things on earth, man alone is capable of considering such questions as the meaning of the universe, or life, or his own existence. Despite the fact that man, like other life on our planet, seems unworthy of consideration when compared to the vastness of the universe, the fact is that man alone can think beyond time to eternity and beyond space to infinity.

While this is an obvious statement, it has important significance for us. Because we as human beings can know the meaning of life as well as the realities of the universe, we are capable of making life into something bigger than it is. Compared to people who live out their days without thinking of anything, those who contemplate life's meaning enrich themselves beyond words.

The French philosopher Blaise Pascal (1623-62) also wrestled honestly with this problem, just as you have. The result of that struggle was his conclusion in the *Pensées* that "Man is but a reed, . . . but he is a thinking reed." Viewed from the perspective of the universe, man is really little larger than nothing, like a particle of dust. But man is

infinitely larger than the atom, or than elementary particles or the smallest units of matter in them. If we compare him to the eternal macrocosm, of course, man's life seems a mere moment, but from the viewpoint of the millisecond life of many elementary particles, his life seems an eternity.

Pascal emphasized the meaning of man's existence as viewed from the enormity of the macrocosm. From this viewpoint, man is certainly a frail being, a reed drifting in a river. But the philosopher does say that man is a reed that *can think*. Thus we can assent to a number of aspects in Pascal's thinking. From my own standpoint, however, I certainly do not agree that man has a reed-like fragility.

Philosophers from ancient India argued that if we inquire into the basic truths of the universe and of man, we find that both converge on the same point. That is, to present the essentials of their conclusion, the rhythms of both the universe and of man are grounded in identical laws. Consequently, though we talk of the macrocosm as something outside of man, we can consider it basically as having been imprinted on the life of every single human being. These philosophers thought, moreover, that man's existence continues eternally; it is as immortal as the universe itself.

Philosophically, these conclusions deal with an important problem. Without going into endless detail, it boils down to this: the universe is not something that stands outside of human life and is antagonistic to it, but both the universe and man have absolutely the same ground of being.

We distort this fact when we think of man and universe as separate entities. If we follow Pascal's description of the universe as a river and man as a reed in it, we find that the river takes on the nature of a fearfully powerful current. But that is not the case. These Indian philosophers did not regard man as separate from but as part of the river of the universe — he is one of its currents.

A single drop of seawater contains every ingredient in the ocean. This drop, moreover, can be expanded infinitely into the seven seas. In the same way, man — minute as he is — has within him the ingredients of the macrocosm; he is provided with the same "functions" as the universe. It is as though one small individual life were magnificent enough to embrace the entire macrocosm.

I suppose my response has become a bit theoretical. Nevertheless, doesn't this discussion suggest the answer to your question? By discovering that in "such a small creature" as yourself you have a being with every potential of the universe, aren't you challenged to find how you might develop that potential? And might we not say that here is an answer to the significance of man's (indeed, of your) existence? It seems to me that the meaning of each individual human life, put in other terms, lies in the improvement of life.

Anybody who is convinced of the unlimited latency in each individual (as part of the infinite macrocosm) will tirelessly attempt to develop himself. The most meaningful sort of human existence, in other words, is the kind which opens up man's potential to life's infinite possibilities.

QUESTION:

One of my friends says, "Flowers are not alive," but I think they are. Yet when he asks me what life is I'm not too sure. Please discuss this problem for me.

ANSWER:

Despite the fact that it is closer than anything to us, there is no word more vague than *life.* Perhaps the clash of ideas referred to in your question stems from this vagueness and the different ways you and your friend use the word "life."

Speaking biologically, we generally treat animals as well as plants as living things. In that sense, then, we can say that even flowers have life, as you suggest. The difference is that animals can move at will while plants cannot. In order to make the difference between them clear, it is convenient to talk as though plants were not living things. That may be the sense in which your friend made his statement.

Now let me try to explain what I think life is. As I am not a specialist in biology, however, I'll have to take a very common-sense approach.

To begin with, all animals, including man, can behave in response to an act of their will. Lower forms of animal life (like an amoeba), however, are almost indistinguishable from plants. Nevertheless, plants do breathe, develop and propagate, so it is conceivable, as just stated, that they have life. But there is this fact to consider. Among the lowest orders of living things are organisms which defy classification. Are they animate or inanimate? At times they act like bacteria. At other times they seem to be minerals.

By analyzing the substances out of which men and animals are made, moreover, we ultimately arrive at chemical elements and atoms, neither of which seems animate. In short, a human being is chemically no different from plants and inanimate things. What is exceptional is that his elements and atoms are arranged in a different manner.

Additionally, humans eat plants and animals to maintain life. As even these animals subsist on plants, the net result is that man's food consists primarily of plant life. But plants grow by absorbing air, water and energy from the sun. Furthermore, you also know that the remains of animals decompose and provide nourishment for plants.

Looking at it this way, perhaps we can make the following conclusion. While we conventionally differentiate between animate and inanimate things, a truly strict division between them is quite difficult. We can also say that when humans, animals, plants and inanimate things interact with one another, their relationship is mutually supportive — now using, now depending on each other.

The next point becomes more difficult. When we carefully observe the natural world in this way, we find that every single thing in the universe seems basically similar.

This is what encourages me to think that there is life in everything. Keep in mind the following facts: (1) in the very beginning, living things came about on our earth when it was a world of inanimate objects; (2) this life gradually evolved into the flora and fauna we have now. Granting these facts, isn't it conceivable that, even when earth was no more than a celestial sphere millions of years in the past, this "inanimate" planet was in effect a gigantic source of life? And isn't it conceivable that earth was pregnant with the structures which eventually sprouted into life, such as plants and animals? Or rather should I say that I think the universe itself, which spawned our planet, is a majestic and throbbing entity which will produce life everywhere if only conditions are right.

The life I speak of here is not the same as that possessed

by those living things we call men or animals. Rather is it the regular rhythms lurking in every basic element — rhythms which bring forth autonomous life. As is the case with vegetation, even though you have a mere inorganic substance or something incapable of deciding where it will move, whenever certain conditions are met, this substance has the potential to create life able to move about on its own. I prefer to describe this as the "dormant life" in all things. Though there are differences between such dormant life and life already activated, I wonder (if you consider that everything existing in the macrocosm is as "alive" as we are) whether we might not say that the universe itself is actually a magnificently unfolding drama of life?

Thus life is not limited to earth. Rather can it be considered something which, given the appropriate environment, will appear and is now appearing everywhere in the universe. In actuality, this idea is something which nearly all scientists support.

In answering the question, "Do flowers have life?" I have gotten far afield. But by dealing with life on such a grand scale it is possible to grasp anew all of nature and the vegetable world in terms of the same living bodies that human beings are. Beyond that, I think we can also perceive how precious and how wonderful *life* is.

Once we agree to that, we'll probably be able to open our eyes to much more profound insights regarding the nature of man himself.

QUESTION:

Everyone must die sometime. What happens to people after death?

ANSWER:

This is one of the most difficult of difficult questions. The root of much human anxiety lies in the uncertainty of its answer.

Well, what happens after a man dies? In the physical sense, if he is cremated he turns to smoke and ashes and merges with the air and the earth. Even consciousness, memory and thought processes disappear. Thus might we not say that on dying everything about a person vanishes?

In our day, this seems to be the universally accepted view. But if death is the absolute end to human life, we are left with a number of things one cannot explain. To begin with, if death is the end it would mean that there is no need to work hard; you could just spend life having fun and enjoying yourself. People would imagine it ridiculous to work oneself to the bone, and they would find honesty a handicap. Present-day trends of thought in large measure seem dominated by this view. I believe that such ideas exert no small influence on the notion that death is the end of human life.

That raises another unexplainable problem. It is amazing how many dissimilarities exist among human beings right *from birth.* Some are born with sound bodies, some are born crippled. Some are born in comfortable and some in destitute homes. Why do these dissimilarities exist? You might answer that the child was born to such-and-such parents and so what can you do about it? But this hardly explains why the baby was born into that particular family.

If we think along these lines, it seems to me that a doubt creeps into the picture. Could there be defects in the notion that there is nothing after death?

Buddhism, arising in India and perfected in Japan, has this to say about the problem. While it is true that the body and the mind perish with death, human life itself continues eternally; death is definitely not the end of man's life.

This may seem an incomprehensible philosophical statement which you cannot readily grasp. It may be easier to get hold of if we look at this Buddhist teaching in terms of the life cycle of water.

Rain water flows into streams. The streams flow into larger rivers and eventually empty into the sea. Everyone understands this process. The same water that fell on the ground as rain turns into sea water. Then water in the sea evaporates and becomes vapor in the atmosphere. We cannot tell merely by observation, however, that this vapor cools and becomes rain again to water the earth. We know this because we have learned it as part of our scientific understanding of the world.

We can compare this recurring cycle to a man's life. We might liken birth to the rain that falls on the earth, death to the evaporation of water from the surface of the sea. Although this is how we would see it with the naked eye, in actuality that is by no means the end of the water. We know that it recycles constantly.

Moreover, whether it is water in rain, in streams or in the sea, or even in the form of ice or vapor, the basic nature of the water is constant: it remains H_2O. Regardless of what external shape or form it assumes, water's basic composition remains the same.

It is the same with human beings. Like the water, people undergo change second by second as their old cells are constantly replaced by new ones. As we pass through infancy, youth and old age, we remain the same human being although *physically* we have been so "rebuilt" that, in a sense, we are not at all the same person.

It is similar in the psychological area, too. Our thinking changes almost completely and continues to shift from time to time. It changes precisely like rain water that flows into the stream and pours finally into the sea.

And yet, the reason we can say that Mr. X remains Mr. X at all times is that his basic nature — that is to say, his *life* — has not in the least changed. It is uniform throughout his span of years. Perhaps we can liken this fact to the basic nature of water, which is a constant H_2O.

The late Dr. Richard E. Coudenhove-Kalergi, the famed proponent of European unity, said something quite similar when I talked with him several years back. Roughly, his opinion was that, from the Western point of view, life can be compared to a book. When you finish reading it, that is the end. The Asian view, however, regards human life as one page in the book. Even after you finish reading that page, new pages follow one after the other.

In the same way, our next life is a continuation of our present life. This view explains some of the problems mentioned at the outset. For example, distinctions between the man who died doing good and one executed for murder will clearly appear in their next existence. It is very much like the chess game which you decided to continue the next day. Everything on the board remains as it was. The pieces you lost or gained the day before are the same. The difficulties you found yourself in when you decided to postpone the game have not changed. If we assume that life itself is similar, don't you think this offers a neat and consistent explanation for why people are born with so many dissimilarities?

These are the reasons I think that death is certainly not

the end of our existence but the beginning of a new life. I would like to urge you to consider the implications of this view. Don't you think that you can live life more constructively, more meaningfully and more vigorously if you take this view than if — regarding human life as limited to its present existence in the world — you lived this life as though it were only a moment?

QUESTION:

Is a person's destiny determined from birth? If so, and if he has bad fortune, can he change it?

ANSWER:

You might say that a person's fortune is more or less determined. From the moment of birth, we find distinctions among human beings; or we find that life will not go the way we wish. Some people fail no matter how hard they strive. Others reap unexpected success without exerting much effort at all. They seem blessed with good fortune.

The outcome is neither determined — nor can it be determined — merely by the will or the way you think. Lying, as it were, external to what can be desired, fate affects life on a grand scale. Whether we call it destiny, fate or whatever, there is a sense in which good or bad fortune has been determined.

Nevertheless, I certainly do not wish to suggest either that everything is determined by our destiny, or that because our fate has been decided we need not keep trying to change it. After all, no matter how favorable one's fortune, he cannot reap where he has not sowed. And no matter how unfavorable one's fortune, he will somehow reap rewards where he has exerted efforts to change his luck. Nor is there reason to think that a person's fate is so predetermined that he is destined to go to a specific school or enter a certain profession.

Fate has the power to influence our fortune, good or bad, in a most crucial manner. We might compare it to the itinerary of a migratory bird, a more-or-less set route from which the bird does not deviate.

That brings us to your second question, "Can we alter our fortune?" Before you can answer that for yourself, you must first of all give thought to what causes fate. Unless you understand the reasons for good or bad fortune, it is not possible to understand how to change it.

What determines fate? Most people apparently think that fortune is a matter of happenstance, of chance. Although every result has some specific cause, laymen often regard results as mere accidents. This resembles the situation in which the trained eye of the scientist views a phenomenon as an obvious outcome of known processes, whereas the untrained eye of the layman might view it as mysterious. But is it not somewhat odd to imagine results without something to produce them, to conceive of fate without a cause?

If cause is important, we must ask what causes our fortune. Actually, this is terribly difficult to do. It is a question which even modern science finds trying to clarify. In order to arrive at a solution, we must view the problem from a fresh perspective, a view not provided either by the average lay or the scientific view.

I have already revealed what that perspective is. At least I offered clues concerning it when I discussed man's relationship to nature and the universe, and when I dealt with the problem of life after death. As stated then, I am convinced that the key to the problem of influencing our fate and changing our fortune lies in the philosophical realm: we must start with a profound respect for, and a desire to work to preserve, human life.

This is no doubt something for you to look carefully into as you mature. Once you have a clear notion of what kind of activities create man's fortune, I feel certain that you will be able to discover how to challenge and change your personal destiny.

My discussion has gotten quite abstract, I suppose. Yet, from what I have said to this point, I hope you will be clear at least on these points. While each and every individual's fortune may be determined, it is possible through your own efforts to turn your fate around and make it move in a favorable direction.

QUESTION:

What do you think is most important for young people to work for?

ANSWER:

Young people are wonderful. They have dreams, they have hopes. They have the potential of young bamboo, growing persistently into the sky. They have the youthful vigor to transform this chaotic and unhappy society into one in which everyone can be happy and satisfied. What is important for young people, it seems to me, is to mature vigorously, to ride over the rough waves of life.

If young people can do that, then I would like to say that the most important thing for them, what they must never lose, is a sense of what is right. I want young people to be the kind of human beings who hold fast to what they believe true, no matter who stands against them.

William Gladstone (1809-98), a famous British statesman, was prime minister four times and a great man who was repected for his learning and personal integrity. When he was at Eton preparing for college, an uproar developed among the students regarding a strike. This occurred when one student had stirred up the entire student body against a teacher he hated. Gladstone alone stood fast and opposed the idea of striking on the ground that hate was not sufficient cause for a strike. Gladstone's classmates concentrated their criticism on the fact that he should be obliged to follow the majority opinion. Among those who opposed him were some ruffians, too, but he never wavered in his determination. In the end, I understand that his opposition prevented the strike.

I do not wish to suggest that Gladstone's attitude on this issue can be applied to every situation. Much rather is it the normal thing to follow the decision of the majority. But in this case the majority decision had not been arrived at after a proper and exhaustive discussion. In Japan, where we have the saying "Yield to those with power," when someone with authority asks us to do something we comply even if we think the request a bit irrational. That is a pathetic state of affairs!

I prefer that young people, who will bear the burdens of the future, hold fast to what they think is right. I think that people who make the most splendid human beings are those capable of standing up for their principles with dignity in everything they do.

Next to a sense of justice, the most important quality is courage. In fact, it is the other side of justice, for no matter how strong one's sense of right, that sense cannot be realized without courage.

Gladstone's courage enabled him to put his sense of justice into practice and to end talk of a strike. Had he thought he was helpless standing alone, had he not courageously put forth the reasons for his opposition, even though he opposed the strike in his heart he would not have been able in actuality to stop it.

Note, however, that courage unsupported by a sense of justice is mere foolhardiness. I suppose one might say that the student trying to start the strike had a kind of courage, too. But it was more misconceived than genuine. At any school, you can find those who have the courage to stand up before others and take the lead. But if they assume leadership for selfish reasons, and if they lead others into doing things that are not right, you could hardly call them courageous.

A sense of justice and true courage lead to a sense of responsibility. Or rather might one say that only a person with a vigorous feeling of responsibility will be likely to develop a sense of justice and courage.

Take the case of a class leader, for example. If such a person has a strong sense of responsibility to improve the class, I am sure he will be an example to all by supporting whatever the class members decide on. Should someone go against a rule all have approved, the exemplary leader will warn him of his error. That is what it means to stand by your feeling for the right, and to stand by it in this manner amounts to a courageous act. Those without a sense of responsibility are bound to pretend they do not notice someone who is acting improperly.

Although I have been talking about justice, courage and responsibility, you should realize that these take many forms. Among the various possibilities, I would like to suggest that the noblest kind of justice, courage and responsibility stands up for human life and defends it as being more important than anything else in the world.

This type is superior, I think, because it is possible to build a solid foundation for peace and happiness, for liberty and equality, on the basis of respect — respect that puts humanity before everything, believing that human life is sacred.

The most important thing for everyone, but above all for the young, is to work for precisely that sense of justice, that courage, that feeling of responsibility.

QUESTION:

There are good people and bad people in the world. We all share the same humanity, so why are some humans good and some bad?

ANSWER:

Philosophers of every age have given much thought to the problem of whether man by nature is basically good or bad. Typically, there are two opposing interpretations. One view stresses the idea that man by nature is fundamentally good; the theory of *innate goodness* holds that it is only through a variety of accidents that badness crops up.

The other viewpoint stresses the idea that man by nature is essentially bad; the theory of *innate badness* holds that only by suppressing man's evil tendencies through laws and discipline is it possible to keep evil in check. Wherever the theory of innate goodness has been adopted, you are likely to find a stress on morality. Wherever the theory of innate badness is highly regarded, it becomes necessary to have strict laws and discipline to help corral man's evil tendencies.

Despite these theories, however, we still end up as you have said with good and bad people. Or rather might one say that the good are not from the outset *completely* good or the bad *completely* bad. Even a person whom we call virtuous on occasion betrays his inner desire for fame and honor or other selfish concerns; and even the arch villain will display tender affection toward his children.

You probably know the famous Robert Louis Stevenson novel, *Dr. Jekyll and Mr. Hyde* (1886). This is the story of how Dr. Jekyll, a dignified and gentle man in the daytime, made a complete switch at nighttime into the wicked Mr. Hyde. Could it be that human beings are endowed from birth with — that they have within themselves — the opposing personalities seen in Jekyll and Hyde?

What I mean is that any human being not only shows an ignoble tendency to trap others, quarrel with them or fawn over them, but at the same time has the noble tendency to forget about saving his own skin and to help somebody in trouble. Either tendency lies dormant. It is not forced out of an individual but surfaces through a variety of accidents at any given moment. I wonder whether this is not the way it really is with people?

If, then, all men have both good and bad tendencies in their character, why do some seem virtuous and some wicked? Education and environment do, to be sure, exert a considerable influence on character. We can easily conceive, for example, that a person who has been raised in poverty-stricken surroundings would tend to develop a personality intent on surviving even if it means trampling over the other fellow.

On the other hand, however, a person who has struggled through life has a clear understanding of what people who struggle must suffer. He will consequently be inclined to lend them a hand. Someone who has never had to struggle through life might rather tend to lord it over those who have struggled, for he would be unfamiliar with the subtle psychology of such people.

Even with those raised in the same environment, moreover, you find some who utilize their surroundings in order to build their character, and you find others who succumb and let their surroundings warp their personalities. When that happens, the problem narrows down to the specific individual involved and not to the nature of the environment.

Of course I do not mean to suggest that you should assume the air of a virtuous person as you deal with your problems. The upshot of that tactic — of acting as though you were virtuous without acknowledging the truth that the potential for both goodness and badness exists within you — would be the sort of split personality evident in Dr. Jekyll and Mr. Hyde.

It is vital that you take a good hard look at yourself. Try to improve your strong points, your special virtues. This is not a matter of ignoring the unsightly and naughty aspects of your character, but of identifying them clearly and getting them under control. Through your accumulated efforts in this direction, the unwholesome aspects of your nature will gradually shrink away and the wholesome aspects will come to the fore.

Although it is easy to talk about "goodness," the standards for judging it are vague. In general, it seems that an exemplary individual who is gentle and modest fits the pattern of a "good person." But I would like to add a few characteristics to that list. The most virtuous person is, I think, one who considers the happiness of others, who loves peace in his society and in the world, who respects life above everything.

No matter how gentle a person, I cannot regard him as a truly good individual unless his objective is to be bold in challenging the unhappiness he sees in the world around him. The truly virtuous person is one who, despite minor faults of character, is constantly prepared to take courageous action in order to achieve that objective.

QUESTION:

Having to listen to our parents and teachers, and having all kinds of restrictions on our activities, we don't enjoy much freedom. Grownups have freedom, why can't we?

ANSWER:

When I was young I had the same thoughts about this problem as you. For I, too, figured that it was a handicap to be a child who is always told, "Don't do that," or "Do this." And I also thought that since grownups have freedom, when I grew up I'd be able to do anything I wanted. But now I can look back on those youthful thoughts with nostalgia.

Certainly, as your question suggests, at first glance it does seem that children lack freedom. But the question is, what does one mean by *freedom?* Before deploring the fact that one lacks freedom, it is necessary to have a firm grasp of what it means.

Many people imagine that freedom means doing what they please. That is a mistake. Doing what one pleases is *license,* not freedom at all. License means doing precisely what one pleases, irrespective of how it inconveniences others. By contrast, freedom is necessarily accompanied by responsibility. Only by behaving with a strict sense of responsibility is it possible to insist on having freedom.

That is why those indifferent to inconveniencing other people, or those incapable of standing by what they have done, have no right to talk about freedom. You probably have an acquaintance or two who insist on their freedom at the drop of a hat, but can you say that they have never mistaken freedom for license?

An example may make my meaning clear. Junior high students have to go to school. At first glance it seems as though your freedom is limited, for after all adults need not attend school. If white-collar workers do not like their jobs they can choose to try whatever they want. Adults do have the responsibilities, however, of supporting families and contributing to the development of society. From the viewpoint of junior high students, adults may appear to have freedom; but from the viewpoint of the adult, children not only have few responsibilities, they seem to have it easy — with rather more freedom than adults.

Parents and teachers very likely drive you young people

to distraction, constantly urging you to keep at your books. I imagine, too, that adults sometimes scold you severely. That may be why you think that children have no freedom. But it is precisely because parents and teachers are responsible for fashioning you into upstanding adults that they scold you and keep after you to study. If you consider the weight of that responsibility, adults certainly do not enjoy the freedom you seem to imagine.

It is easy to state that freedom is accompanied by responsibility. Beyond that statement, however, it is necessary to arm oneself with the capability of discharging his responsibilities in order to acquire freedom. At the moment you and your friends may find your life constricted. But as you are being forced to obey your parents and teachers, you are being disciplined in the ability to discharge your responsibilities.

This discipline might be compared to small boats in which sailors learn navigation under the supervision of a training ship. No matter how much the sailors in the small boats — lacking compass and navigation techniques as well as the full capabilities of the mother ship to sail the open sea — would like to run about unrestricted, were they to do so they would doubtlessly end up on the ocean floor.

That is why, as you can see, the sailors must acquire navigational skills, as they must acquire the ability to negotiate heavy seas, and they must learn to make judgments that allow them to anticipate and weather danger *before* they are allowed to sail large ships. Until their discipline is complete, sailors have to use the smaller boats under the watchful eye of the mother ship to train themselves for the day they can venture alone onto the high seas.

And so you should not see the things your parents and teachers tell you as obligations. Rather should you regard them as opportunities for you to master responsibility at this stage in your life. I would like to see you commit yourself to this long-range objective: develop adequate skills so that you will eventually be able to sail the high seas of society to your heart's content and, incidentally, contribute to the peace and happiness of all people. If you have such a firm sense of direction, you may see that complaining about restrictions is petty.

Looking at the problem from another angle, I might suggest that, compared to grownups, I do not really think junior high students lack freedom. During vacations, on holidays and after classes you have periods of time which you may use as you like; isn't that a far greater amount of leisure than adults have? You can enjoy yourselves in those periods through sports, reading books you like, listening to music and so forth. You are altogether free, too, during those hours you play with your friends. So now, when you are in junior high, you can freely do all sorts of things that you cannot do as freely when you grow up.

Certainly you have a number of restrictions on your activities. I doubt, for example, that any teacher would approve of your roaming the streets at night or fooling around downtown after dark.

It seems to me, however, that an answer to your query lies somewhere between the following questions. Should you complain that your present restrictions rob you of freedom? Or should you regard yourself as a trainee trying actively to do everything you can to sail the high seas on your own?

QUESTION:

Whenever I read about great men, I get the feeling that I have it too good now. How can a person perfect himself under present-day circumstances? And could you define a "great man"?

ANSWER:

We say that adversity makes us wise. This means that we need not avoid adversity and hardship, for only by challenging and overcoming them can we perfect ourselves and become complete human beings. There are many stories about those who faced hardship in their youth but overcame it and ended up heroes or famous people with our respect and confidence. When reading of such people, you most likely imagine that your lack of economic hardships or family distress prevents you from imitating the great.

To be sure, your circumstances are quite different from those of the great people you have read about. Or are they? Try reading those passages again. Is it really true that these people attribute their development to the experience of having been subjected to hardships? There are countless examples of people in distressful circumstances, many of whom I am sure have surrendered to their surroundings, gone astray and lived out their lives as defeated beings. Ultimately the question is not one of environment at all but of the person's attitude toward it. In the great, a determination to challenge and overcome one's circumstances is more powerful than in average people. I regard this as the outstanding characteristic of a great man.

Human beings are not *determined* by their environment. What they become is determined by how they *use* their environment. That is why it is absolutely inappropriate to think that, because at this moment your circumstances are favorable, you have no chance to perfect yourself as a human being. If only you have the determination to improve yourself, you can discover the means to do so all about you. It is not a matter of what your circumstances are. The issue is rather how you deal with them. In fact, I might even suggest that the mere notion your circumstances are too favorable, that you therefore lack the stimulus for growth, suggests you may already have surrendered to them.

You can begin to perfect yourself right where you are. For example, you must know somebody who is alienated, who stands alone, someone ready to abandon hope. Why not endeavor to become the fast friend of such a person, helping him recover his joy in life? If you can give that a try, you will very likely discover it to be one of the toughest of tough things to accomplish. But the moment you take courage and make an effort to carry out your plan, you will be actively involved in perfecting yourself.

And yet it is true that, undercurrents aside, in these days Japan is comparatively tranquil and settled. These are not, in other words, days of change and upheaval as, for example, those our nation experienced following the Meiji Restoration (1868) or in the aftermath of World War II. Consequently, it may not be quite proper at this time to talk of the sort of spectacular international political arena where the great have performed in history.

In my opinion, however, the ranks of the great are by no means limited to those who participate bodily on the stage of history, enjoying the tumultous applause of vast audiences. I also find it difficult to imagine that a man can be called "great" or a hero — despite whatever notable leadership capabilities he might display and despite the new age he might create — if in the final analysis his leadership drives people into wars and forces them to shed their blood.

What is a truly great man? — He does not have to be

famous. He does not have to leave his name in history books. In my judgment he is, as it were, the sort of person who would warmly embrace some unhappy old woman (beyond being helped by riches or power or technology) in order to end her afflictions and deliver her from her problems.

It makes no difference how far advanced a civilization may be or how many physical conveniences it provides. No amount of material possessions can soften the sort of anguish one feels as a human being. I might even go so far as to say that the more advanced and developed a civilization, the more unhappy its people. One viewpoint is that the superficial prosperity of our age only increases the fundamental afflictions which we experience as human beings. In such an age, therefore, the noblest sort of human being is the one who, willing to embrace the sorrows of his neighbor, acts in order to create a truly peaceful and happy society.

I would like you and all young people like you, all those who will be the next generation of leaders, to become just such noble human beings. To accomplish that end, I think you'll have to begin right now to discipline yourselves, to absorb knowledge and furnish yourselves with the skills you will need for that day.

Whether studying, participating in student organizations and extracurricular activities, or solving problems that arise with your friends, you have endless occasions to improve yourself. I sincerely trust that you will positively search out opportunities for improvement and that you will challenge life squarely so that you might mature into an outstanding individual.

QUESTION:

Men and women have different ideas on the matter, but would you mind telling me what you think are the characteristics of the ideal woman?

ANSWER:

Following World War II, the notion of the equality of the sexes gradually spread through Japanese society. This resulted in publication of a great number of books describing the ideals of the "new woman."

I prefer leaving specialized matters to such books and to convey to you — by way of responding to your question — my own everyday feelings on the matter. In frankly reporting exactly what's on my mind, my words may seem more directed to adults than to you. Since these opinions could be of use to you in the future, however, please try to bear with me.

We should rejoice that the status of women has recently been on the rise throughout our society. Compared to the days when women had no choice but to spend their lives obeying men, this represents tremendous progress. We might even call it a revolution.

Nevertheless, I do have certain qualms about the demand to put women on exactly the same footing as men just because the female has so long been downgraded in Japan. This demand, evident among certain elements of the movement for women's liberation and "woman power," insists on looking to men as the standards for women. There are instances where this demand actually causes antagonism between the sexes. But doesn't all this shouting about *Women! Women!* betray a sense of personal inferiority?

It is for that reason that I expect the following of every woman. Rather than debate her views on being a *woman,* it is more important to talk of being *human*. In short, before asking how one might better exist as a *woman*, ask how one might better exist as a *person*. To become a splendid person is of itself the highest ideal for any woman. Beyond that it seems to me that women should be advised to make the most of their distinctive qualities as women and to give full play to their strong points.

There are actually some in the radical camp who, in aiming to become men's equals in every area, take the extreme position of detesting their own distinctively female qualities. I cannot help thinking that this attitude, which clearly disdains women's strong points, suggests how radicals have become entranced by the *forms* of equality but have forgotten what equality itself is all about.

Men have characteristics which women do not have. Women, in turn, have special characteristics which men do not have. True equality is not a matter of women imitating men but of women making the most of their own special characteristics, something which no man can possibly imitate. At the same time, true equality is also a matter of overcoming the special defects common to the female species. In sum, these are, we might say, appropriate and natural ideals.

Let me be a bit more concrete on this latter point. To begin with, a girl ought to be a modern woman, well furnished with a sense of her own personality. Or rather I would prefer that she always be a positive, cheerful person with her own sense of autonomy, and that she assuredly stand above being forced to conform now to this fashion, now to that social trend.

Next, I would like women to take a broad view of society and to consider problems from a long-range perspective. Most young girls will eventually get married. I hope that they will always jealously maintain a broad perspective on affairs so that, instead of becoming shut up in the narrow confines of their families, they will become actively engaged with others in society and aggressively deal even with political and economic issues. I also think it would be ideal for women to have the pluck to travel widely, not merely in Japan but into the world at large.

It is, furthermore, my hope that women might be filled with good judgment, that they might have the ordinary wisdom to create the more abundant life and, more than anything, that they might become individuals filled with vitality and wholesomeness.

This list of ideals may somehow seem quite commonplace. That hardly matters because, as far as I am concerned, nothing is more wonderful than living fully as a common citizen. And, actually, what is more difficult than living a truly human life?

The mere presence of a cheerful woman will brighten and restore perspective to everyone around her. I cannot refrain from hoping, therefore, that each and every young girl might mature into an honest and vivacious individual, one who brightens her school, her home and her community — one who is adored by all.

Moreover, I would like each junior high girl to become the sort of individual who can take into adulthood an earnest appeal for world peace. If the entreaties of young girls imbued with the noble privilege of nourishing and safeguarding life were to spread over the entire face of our globe, then world peace — long the ideal of all mankind — would most certainly become a reality.

QUESTION:

I've recently become interested in sex and I've been talking about it with my friends. Is it wrong to think and talk about such things?

ANSWER:

I suspect that sex is something almost everyone your age thinks about. When I was as old as you, our country was at war and people regarded it as indecent to think and talk about sex. Nowadays sex education is debated, various books on sex have been published, and we're able to talk about it quite frankly. I find this a desirable trend.

In Japan, however, sex continues to be used more often than not merely to titillate. And unlike European countries, we fall short of making sincere efforts to provide the younger generation with proper knowledge about sex. That is probably why young people like yourself acquire distorted ideas on the topic from friends or certain magazines, and why you actually doubt whether you should even think of such things.

Regarding the question of sex and sex education, Japan is at present in a transitional period. On the one hand, the old-fashioned Confucian moralistic rule that boys and girls should not sit together after the age of seven remains deeply rooted among the people, as does the easy-going notion that children will naturally learn about sex without our teaching them all these new-fangled ideas about it. The results of such notions, one might say, include thinking that sex is filthy and disgusting, having an extreme sense of guilt about it, and slipping into an attitude of being pervertedly morbid about it. And because people have such notions, vulgar and mistaken information persists in circulating in a hush-hush way. Countless tragedies have occurred because of such misunderstandings.

On the other hand, in conflict with these deeply-rooted traditional ideas is a flood of "liberated" sex in certain magazines and movies — sex that has degenerated into nothing more than titillating commercialism. Affected by this flood, many now advocate an excessive sexual freedom of the sort which is totally unrelated to (and actually destroys) marriage and true love.

From my viewpoint, neither old-fashioned notions nor excessive freedom is the proper way to deal with sex. A natural instinct which man has always possessed, sex itself is definitely nothing to be ashamed of. And, if one regards sex from the viewpoint of the preservation of our species, we must say it is a mistake to think of it merely as a way to enjoy ourselves.

In view of all this, the first thing I'd like to make clear to you is that there is absolutely no need to be distressed by strange feelings of guilt regarding your interest in sex. Obviously, there is nothing to be ashamed of.

If at all possible, I urge you to acquire proper information about sex. Depending on your circumstances, you might make up your mind to ask your folks or a teacher at school. As you talk over the various aspects of the problem, you'll discover that though you label them "questions about sex" you're not really dealing with an uncommon topic at all. When you make that discovery, I imagine you'll feel quite relieved.

The most advisable thing for you now, however, is to pour all your energies into accomplishing the tasks at hand, whether studies or sports or music or whatever. Sexual questions are for grownups to worry about, so no matter how much you think about such problems there is no reason to expect that you can resolve them now. If, rather, you involve yourself enthusiastically in some activity at school, you'll discover that in spite of yourself your current gloomy mood will melt away.

In order for that to happen, you have to grasp firmly what is vital for you at this moment. There is no doubt that sex and love are very important. But there are other things which should be more important for you at this time in your life. Whether studies or extracurricular activities, everything you experience at school constitutes a precious asset for your future; now is the time for you to use those experiences.

Make no mistake that this is the moment of *opportunity* to acquire these assets. Go ahead and begin by building a strong body with tenacious spiritual strength so you may grow into a truly superior person.

QUESTION:

I think everyone should be free and equal. But societies which are free lack equality, and whenever a society attempts to establish equality it seems that freedoms disappear. What's a sensible way to view freedom and equality?

ANSWER:

As you have pointed out — and I agree — people ought to be free as well as equal. I suppose everyone feels the same.

In actuality, however, it is extremely difficult to create a society where that is the case. In contemporary Japan, for example, we have been guaranteed various freedoms, and yet we certainly cannot claim that our people enjoy equality. On a world-wide scale it is possible to say that an identical situation exists, even in the so-called free nations like the United States of America. By contrast, socialist countries like the Soviet Union and China generally emphasize equality for their citizens, but in these lands there are apparently a number of restrictions on the individual's freedom.

The numerous disagreements between the free and the socialist worlds arise from profoundly different ways of thinking about government, economics and society. These differences divide the world. The stress each of these worlds puts on freedom and equality, however, may be said to be the most conspicuous discrepancy between them. A glance at this reality shows us how very difficult it is to establish a society where people enjoy equality as well as freedom.

But just because it is a difficult task is no reason, it seems to me, to imagine that it is impossible to realize. Actually, even the "free nations" have steadily been adopting social welfare systems and helping the old and those with handicaps in an effort to offer every citizen an equal chance. And the socialist countries, for their part, have come to recognize a certain amount of freedom for the individual. These facts alone attest, perhaps, to the earnest world-wide efforts being made to establish a society in which people might enjoy both freedom and equality.

It is not clear to me, however, whether it is possible to achieve an ideal society merely by adopting the strong points from one or the other of the two camps. Even if in theory this is conceivable, since the fundamental concepts of the ideal society differ in either case, I wonder whether the net result might not be like trying to graft a slip of bamboo to an apple tree?

To be sure, as you suggest in your question, freedom and equality are mutually exclusive ways of looking at things. But if you think carefully about the problem, this antagonism stems from the impossibility of achieving harmony between the individual and the group or polity. I mean, when you put the needs of the polity first, you sacrifice the individual's freedom; and when you honor the freedom of the individual, the polity becomes riddled with inequalities.

Now then, the point I wish to make is this. Whether speaking of freedom or equality, we must shift our viewpoint to fundamentals. That is to say, when it comes right down to issues, the view that provides the basis for either freedom or equality is the "dignity of man." Because the human being deserves more respect than any *thing*, I believe that each person must be free; and because all human beings should be respected equally, I believe that every single person must be equal.

If we look at it in this manner, we'll be using the word *equality* properly and not applying it indiscriminately to all sorts of things or external forms. Applying the concept of equality to externals is definitely a distortion of the term. But if we speak from the view that accords ultimate respect to every single individual, certainly the true meaning of equality is to provide equal opportunity to each and every person so he can pursue whatever ends he desires. From the standpoint of each citizen, wouldn't that approach itself actually amount to being free?

Whenever we forget this and seek equality in external forms only — rather than root it in respect for the human being — freedom disappears. And whenever we think that freedom alone is enough, we end up with a society where the weak are devoured by the strong, a situation producing tremendous inequalities.

Concretely, the question of what kind of social system to establish is a problem for statesmen, economists and the like. That is why it is an issue which I'd like you and other concerned young people to think about in the future, beginning from the viewpoint expressed above.

Contemporary society is plagued with contradictions and irrationalities. But you, my young friends, can make an enormous contribution by figuring out how these might be reduced. I eagerly and sincerely await the application of your insights to these problems.

QUESTION:

We have different races, we have rich and poor, etc. — there are all kinds of differences among people. I think that everyone was originally equal, but how come all these differences arise?

ANSWER:

There are of course various kinds of differences among people. It is not possible to deal with all of them so I have decided to limit my response to the problems of race and poverty which you have asked about.

As stated earlier, fundamentally every person must be equal. That is the basic premise of my own policy and of all that I advocate; it is my firm belief that this is the way things must be.

And yet, having said that, I still cannot deny the fact that differences among people do exist. We must confront this reality head on and, on the basis of our confrontation, consider how such differences came about and how we might eradicate them. Then we must summon the courage to work for a solution to the problem.

To begin with is the problem of racial discrimination. It is anthropologically untenable that differences in skin coloration, whether black or yellow or white, make people superior or inferior or denote differences in ability. Such views are assuredly groundless, mistaken concepts. Using external differences to distinguish among Anglo-Saxons, Germans, Slavs, and people of Mongolian blood is simply a handy means of classifying people for academic purposes. The "special characteristics" of these peoples exist on the same level as distinctions between those who are short or tall, fat or thin.

The arch criminal that has turned external features into a means of discrimination is, in my opinion, "education." For

example, whenever one race or nation conquers an indigenous people, the conquerors' sense of superiority over the natives eventually surfaces in the notion that they had been a superior race all along. The most obvious yardstick of their superiority is difference in skin color. This attitude is passed from generation to generation as a kind of inheritance. That is to say, in the process of being educated, a child becomes filled with a sense of superiority based on nothing more than differences in skin pigmentation.

It seems to me that this is why something like racial discrimination (the sense of superiority Europeans felt when they conquered Indians in the New World or Americans' feelings of contempt for the Africans they had enslaved) survives to this day as a sense of superiority which takes many forms. The reason racial discrimination is comparatively weak in Japan might be due to the fact that the Japanese have not received such "education."

Looking at the problem in this way, we can see that if we wish to eliminate racial discrimination it will be necessary to continue doggedly — in school, in the home, and in society — to educate people to the belief that all men are equal. As a matter of fact, while abroad I have often seen Blacks and Whites arm in arm singing songs and talking together, for they had learned to think that all people are fundamentally equal.

The other part of your question concerns differences between the rich and the poor. This is an extremely annoying problem. At this moment the world is divided into two antagonistic camps, socialism and capitalism. It may be appropriate to suggest that the basic source of that antagonism, not to mention the problem of freedom and equality just touched upon, lies in the differing ways in which people think about the question of the gulf between rich and poor.

Of course, it is desirable that everyone have an equal amount of wealth, that there be no distinctions between rich or poor. The world probably has no choice but to move toward that ideal in the future. But all the same, I think it questionable whether socialism as we see it today is the answer. What I mean is that with an equal distribution of wealth, one fears there will no longer be objectives to work for; we could end up with a society of sluggards. In the Soviet Union, we have seen privately owned farms out-producing communally owned lands. Consequently, it will be difficult indeed to solve this problem. But we simply must conceive of methods to wipe out the distinctions between rich and poor without robbing people of the will to work.

I hope no one will misconstrue my point. It is a mistake to imagine that everything will be solved if only we institute the proper social system and government organs. Each and every human being has his own individuality and the desire for freedom. If, however, we merely push for our own equality, we'll only be able to move into a kind of authoritarianism which absolutely ignores individuality.

In any case, problems of discrimination and differences among races include a number of questions beyond race, beyond the gulf between rich and poor. Certainly, giving consideration to every single aspect of human equality will doubtlessly become one of mankind's most vital future tasks.

QUESTION:

I think that man's greatest misfortune is war, and yet somebody is always at war somewhere on the face of the earth. How do you suppose we can create a peaceful world where there are no wars?

ANSWER:

I truly think that nothing is as miserable, as brutal as war. Or, rather than suggest that this is only a *thought*, I should say I am compelled out of personal experience to make that statement.

That abominable Pacific War began when I was just about your age. One after the other my four big brothers went off to the battlefront for the "noble purpose" of fighting for our country. Even if I try, I shall never forget the pained look in Mother's eyes when each left, or the inexplicable sorrow in her face when she was told a son had died in battle. The grief over losing a beloved son was something my mother shared with other mothers throughout the world.

A disgust for war has thus been carved indelibly into my mind. Along the way this disgust resulted in a pledge that I would dedicate myself to working to make a world without wars.

Even today I feel myself bound to that pledge. I am forced to grieve that human beings, so proud of their lofty intellect as the lords of creation, should for one reason or the other kill each other. Wondering, Why do they do it? fills me with the urge to abolish wars this very instant.

No matter how much one rants against war, however, reality does not change. What we need is to concentrate the good judgment of everyone who loves peace and, joining forces, to exert ceaseless efforts against war.

Now let me turn to some of the reasons that wars occur.

Historically, it seems that there have been various causes for wars. Wars have been waged for such straightforward reasons as the desire to obtain food. Some wars have been fought with the aim of making more complete economic penetration of an area, others in order to satisfy a dictator's lust for conquest. There are, additionally, wars which break out for religious or ideological reasons.

Nevertheless, if one inquires further into the question, we find one most fundamental cause for war: in each case it is the ugly side of man's nature. In the affairs of men, it most often occurs that if one party *takes* the other party *loses*. And it is man's nature to try to acquire more and more if he has taken something, just as he will try to recoup what he has lost. That's the reason quarrels arise. And one party might even end up killing the other should the argument intensify.

The expressions *take* and *lose* may be inappropriate, and there may be aspects of war which cannot be illustrated so simply. But it seems to me all the same that what is common to every cause of war is man's instinctual *greed*.

Everybody knows what is so evil about the fact that human beings kill one another. Yet despite this knowledge, the fact is that wars are constantly being fought somewhere under various pretexts. It might even be appropriate to say that the history of man has been the history of warfare.

Thus we can conclude that human greed is a tremendous demon. Humans have reason. But if man's reasoning powers were sufficiently compelling, there would be no reason for him to wage war. And yet something like logic pales in the face of the demon *Greed;* reason seems about as effective as a small fire extinguisher in putting out a conflagration.

Well, then, how do you suppose we can go about abolishing war? For one thing, I believe we can change our values. I mean we can alter our *awareness* so that everyone becomes conscious of the fact that human life is to be given top priority, that it must be regarded as the most precious thing we have. Or rather should I say that changing our values means more than altering our consciousness. It is a matter of so strengthening and so intensifying our awareness of the value of human life that even our unconscious will constantly be conscious of it!

And then, no matter how glorious a war is made to seem, it could never be justified if it resulted in the loss of even one human being. For everyone would hold tenaciously to the belief that human life is sacred and that any "justification" for taking it is a whitewash.

I would particularly like to appeal to you young people who will be responsible for this world when you become adults. In the past, countless numbers of young men have been spurred to go to war under this or that banner of "righteous" causes. They went off to some hateful battlefield and everyone was reduced to the depths of misery: the youth who had to fight, obviously, but also his parents, his brothers and sisters, his friends, his sweetheart. I would like you all to go through your entire lives with the attitude that war is hell so that, no matter what the circumstances of your time, mankind may nevermore experience such misery.

This is, however, not something you can accomplish merely by making a lot of noise about it. In order to create such an attitude, a person needs a profound philosophy, capable both of taking a penetrating look at the demon of greed which nests in the human heart and of resisting and properly controlling that demon.

One reality of our day is that the philosophy of human respect, humanitarianism or humanism, which is grounded in reason is now suffering a tragic defeat at the hands of this demon Greed. When one gives thought to this fact, I suspect that the only way to shift the balance is to have every single human being come to regard life as something sacred. That will be the conclusive factor in the eradication of war.

Why is life precious? How might we realize perfectly in our lives and in society the ideal that life is our most priceless possession? When we are able to produce a philosophy capable of providing answers to these fundamental questions, man will probably be able to put a stop to his long history of slaughter.

QUESTION:

Science advances these days with tremendous energy, and yet we have serious problems with pollution. What will happen to Japan and to the world in the 21st century?

ANSWER:

It is extremely difficult to surmise what may happen to society in the future. A number of years ago we had a boom in Futurism, and many scholars described the future of society in rosy terms. More recently, however, as we have taken a closer look at the problems of pollution and the like, it seems that more scholars are rather pessimistic in their evaluations. This is why I can say that it is nearly impossible to make accurate suppositions about the future.

Moreover, while it is vital to give thought to what the future might be like, it is even more important to consider the sort of future we are *creating*. The world and Japan of the 21st century are not the responsibility of some vague "somebody." They will belong to you young people who must introspectively devote yourselves to the question of what sort of future age you wish to create.

I have decided to point out in the following paragraphs several problematic issues which may serve as reference material for your thought. My remarks assume, however, that there will be no large-scale conflagration such as World War III, for if such a war broke out it seems that the very survival of mankind — and thus of whether the world might greet a 21st century — would be in doubt.

In the first place, I think no one contests the fact that the 21st century will see the nearly unimaginable development of science and technology. Recent developments in these material aspects of civilization have been astonishing. We have actually viewed on our television screens the

exploration of the moon, something that was little more than a fantastic dream in my own boyhood. Truly, there seems no limit to the extent of scientific progress possible during the nearly three decades left until the 21st century.

What we must consider here, however, is this fact. There is not necessarily a one-to-one relationship between the development of science or technology and the increase of human happiness.

Certainly new technologies in travel and communication have developed markedly, and new products are created one after the other to make our lives incomparably more convenient than they were. Yet, in the end, scientific progress has also resulted in the creation of instruments (like nuclear weapons) capable of instantaneously exterminating mankind.

Of itself science is neither good nor bad. What is crucial is the human being who uses what science produces. Depending on who that person is, science can either make an immeasurable contribution to the promotion of human happiness, or it can develop destructive armaments to wipe out the human race. Obviously, then, in any thinking about the future the dominant theme must necessarily be the problem of man himself.

Secondly is pollution closely linked with scientific advances and a problem which has recently become painfully acute. The situation is indeed so critical that at this moment it may be no exaggeration to claim that our entire environment has become contaminated by poisonous substances, not just our air and our rivers but the sea and the land as well. Moreover, not only are we unable to point to a neat plan capable of solving our pollution problems in a trice, but the more our technology progresses the more dangerous the levels of contamination become. Thus the problem is terribly complex.

We human beings are taking some measures in the face of this grim reality, but as a matter of fact the situation has elicited warnings from many scholars that we may be facing extinction, and if we go on like this some actually predict that the end may come surprisingly soon.

At the moment, pollution in advanced industrial nations like Japan is a particularly thorny problem. When one considers what is happening in Japan — a country where formerly untainted areas (which till recently never gave pollution a second thought) are now being contaminated inch by inch — one becomes apprehensive that the same phenomenon may eventually occur on a world-wide scale.

Thirdly, our lives have been enriched in the material realm and the work week has shrunk. And yet this is perhaps offset by the fear that we are developing a society that has lost sight of the reasons for living. At this very moment, in wealthy lands like the United States of America, many young people have become hippies in order to live in a more *human* way. This arises, perhaps, when young people living in an environment where one can generally get whatever he wants and where much of the work is done by machines begin to have doubts concerning the purpose of life.

The question of the meaning of life is doubtlessly *the* question for mankind. A solution to the problem of what man should be will assuredly be extremely vital in the years ahead.

I could, of course, list more than these three issues. But I wonder whether the most important issue of the 21st century may not be that of "science and man." I also have the feeling that the problem of man himself will be dealt with in a far weightier manner than it has in any past age.

To take a step beyond that, it seems inevitable that we will ultimately be obliged to return to the purely philosophical problem: "Well, how *can* we achieve a proper development of science and a proper understanding of man?" That is why we might well call the 21st century something like "The Century of Philosophy."

On Character

QUESTION:

I'm overly sensitive. Whenever I'm slightly criticized by my friends, even if it's about nothing at all, I get to brooding about it and lose confidence in myself. How can I get some perspective on things?

ANSWER:

Sensitivity in itself is a personality trait. It is not something either good or bad. Scientists, for example, must pay meticulous attention to precision in their experiments. One who is a sensitive person and who makes the most of this trait can turn it into a plus.

Consequently, thinking deeply about something a friend has criticized in you is certainly not in itself bad, nor is it worth fretting about. I think your touchiness indicates that you have both the humility proper to self-reflection and a gentle nature.

On the other hand, indifferent people who pay little attention to anything lack perspective. Those who do not reflect on their behavior despite being corrected, even if the caution was right to the point, should be regarded as irresponsible people deficient in sincerity.

But the most problematic are often those people who do reflect on their behavior when corrected. The trouble is that they immediately brood over trifles. Despite the fact that self-reflection should basically help one mature and grow, some people seem to get upset about examining themselves and withdraw into their shells instead.

You should have more confidence in yourself. To accomplish that, you'll have to keep various problems separate in your thinking: this is one problem, that is another. It is natural for human beings to have faults, so it is foolish to lose confidence in yourself and your strengths just because you admit to a few weaknesses.

Assume, for example, that a friend tells you, "You're always late." Since it is not good to be tardy, you should take the criticism to heart. But even if you do, there is no reason to think that tardiness is the sum total of your whole person. Being late is being late. Your other characteristics are all separate problems — that's how you should take the criticism. In that way, you can balance your weaknesses with your strong points and keep from getting the idea you are hopeless.

In other words, calmly accept the criticism with a positive attitude. If you do that you can decide whether your friend's caution hits the mark or not. And you will also know whether he is genuinely concerned to help you or whether he said it on impulse or because of some misunderstanding.

If you can take this attitude, it will not be particularly necessary to make an issue of criticisms, nor to fret excessively over them. That is to say, if you accept them with a positive attitude, criticisms can help nourish your growth as a person.

Isn't accepting criticism in that way the same as having "some perspective on things"?

My own spiritual guide, Mr. Josei Toda, often told me, "Be a good listener." He meant that people react differently to the same criticism: some will listen to it and lose confidence in themselves, thinking they are hopeless; others will be stimulated by it and use it as a springboard for growth. The latter is the "good listener." I certainly agree. In that regard, don't you think you are selling yourself short?

It is unreasonable to expect to find a person so perfect that he lacks faults. It is even more unreasonable to expect that you yourself might have only a few faults at a time when you are still growing and learning. It makes no difference what people criticize about you now. Just move ahead with composure, feeling certain that sooner or later you will overcome each fault and mature into a splendid person.

QUESTION:

I just can't say what's on my mind in front of others. I'd like to overcome my shyness, but how can I learn to speak up more boldly?

ANSWER:

Young people your age become quite aware of themselves and quite sensitive to their surroundings. It seems to me that nearly everyone at that stage has suffered more or less from the same feelings of shyness you mention. As they mature, however, most acquire the ability to say whatever they think should be said. So I don't think you should at this time worry too much about your shyness.

For somebody like yourself, actually suffering from timidity, this may not seem much of an answer. You want to know, "Isn't there a quick way to remedy my problem?" It might well be done by disciplined training. In a word, you have to work at speaking up before others until it becomes easier.

At first, make up your mind to consider yourself a huge success if you can even say half of what's on your mind. With that attitude, you'll be able to make an honest attempt each and every time the opportunity arises — even if you stumble. There is nothing to feel ashamed about, even should you trip up, because people who can say everything on their minds without a hitch are rare. "If at first you don't succeed, try, try again." We learn to grow by failing. So failure is not something to feel ashamed of. Rather should you despise the attitude that regards failure as a disgrace.

All right, then, the next time you plan to speak be sure to follow this important procedure: Open your mouth only *after* you have clearly thought through and put in order what you want to say. Once you get used to talking before others, you will be able to organize on your feet, your mind working ahead of your words. But in the beginning you may sometimes choke up and your words will not get beyond the tip of your tongue. It might be a good idea to make a few brief notes and to glance at them as you speak.

There will also be times when you try too hard to say something forcefully and fail miserably. One reason some people seem poor at speaking is that they try too hard to be eloquent, despite the fact that they do not believe they have a knack for speaking in front of others. The result is that they completely freeze up. Then they identify freezing up with failing, and failure further undermines their self-confidence. It's a vicious circle. That is why one should not try to be eloquent. It is enough if you endeavor to convey exactly what you have on your mind at the moment. The words will then flow with relative ease.

I've been talking about problems of methodology. But basically, not being able to say what you have in mind is a problem of conviction and courage. What I mean is that if you sincerely think you *must* say something, if you are really convinced of it, your courage naturally will take care of itself. You will not be able to remain silent.

Certainly there are those who can express themselves vigorously, as well as those who do not express themselves too well. You might classify such people as aggressive or passive, though that is a superficial way to look at the problem. After all, it is to some extent a matter of inherited differences in personality. Nor is it necessarily true that people who express themselves vigorously have both courage and conviction. We might rather say that the individual who can offer his opinion when he *must* do so is mature, even if he does not talk up very frequently.

In your case, I hope you will not be satisfied to classify yourself permanently as a shy person. If you say what you believe you must say, and say it with conviction, you will no longer be shy and retiring. Those with such restraint in speaking up before others not only display an extremely important virtue, they also influence people far more than those who talk all the time.

There is no need to imitate the skillful talker. Glib people are not convincing. Even if you do not think you have a gift for speaking in front of a group, the truly convincing talker is the one who firmly gives his points one by one. He need not be eloquent. I would like you to be true to yourself. Be the sort of person who, once he opens his mouth, offers valuable opinions which no one can resist paying attention to.

QUESTION:

I have a short temper and fly off the handle in an instant. Afterwards I always feel sorry about it. How can I change this aspect of my personality?

ANSWER:

Basically, personality is something constant. This opinion may give you the impression that people with short tempers will always have short tempers. But that is not true.

There are two sides to the problem of personality. Take the person with a short temper, for example. Even though rashness itself cannot be regarded as a positive characteristic, on the other hand short-tempered people do tend to be decisive. Their merit is that they are quick to act. Perhaps, then, we can say that when the "bad" side of this personality characteristic turns up we call it "short temper," but when the "good" side turns up it is called "decisiveness" or "the ability to take action."

In a word, personality is like a mountain stream. In the same way that the course of the stream has been determined by the topography, the basic nature of one's character is set. But the flow of the stream is sometimes clear, sometimes muddy. Being short-tempered is when the stream is muddy; when the stream clears up, its "merits" of decisiveness and the ability to act come to the surface. I suspect we can say the same about the problems of being nervous or hesitant about doing things, topics which I have dealt with previously.

So the question is, how can you clear up the short-tempered "muddiness" in the stream of your personality? Of first importance is acquiring a new habit: you must learn to consider problems not just from your own but from the other fellow's viewpoint. This is terribly difficult to do, but flying off the handle at the drop of a hat seems most common in people who look at everything from their own viewpoint. That's why you'll have to make conscious efforts to learn how to curb this tendency in yourself.

How does one learn to do that? Well, you can take a lesson from the old saying that it's a good idea to let a day pass before posting a letter which criticizes somebody. By doing that you have a chance to check later to see — after you've cooled off — whether the letter overstated your case. After all, it is easy for such a letter to get heatedly emotional, and if you send it as is you could end up with quite the opposite result you intended.

Technically, learning to see from the other person's viewpoint is only a matter of being rational. Rationality is the major difference between men and animals. It stands to reason that a person will get angry when he is justly provoked. But getting your dander up over just anything at all is to react very much like an animal. As you youself say, the upshot of your flying off the handle is that in the end you always feel sorry for having done it.

A person forever getting upset about everything cannot arouse sympathy from others, even should he have just cause for his anger. Impulsive anger, even if based on a sense of being in the right, looks to a third-person observer as though the angry individual is shadow boxing. Perhaps the expression "haste makes waste" applies here. A short temper is self-defeating; indeed, it is a great waste. Even if you can get everyone to stand behind you, being up in arms about everything will result in turning your supporters away from you.

Humans are, to be sure, emotional animals. There is no reason to expect anyone to be without feelings. If such a person exists, he would probably be regarded as little better than dead. It is true, moreover, that intense emotion can move the hearts of many people. There are numerous examples in history where a person charged with the sense of being in the right gave a speech that brought listeners to their senses and effected changes in society.

Feelings are therefore extremely important. There is definitely nothing wrong with them. But one's sentiments should be backed up by rationality rather than raw emotion. As the above example of the moving speech illustrates, even if one's heart boils with a sense of righteous indignation, the question is, How can I communicate my indignation to others? We can gain the sympathy of the listener only when we present our case logically and objectively. That is one thing I had in mind when I spoke about being rational and said you should consider problems from the other fellow's viewpoint.

Each individual has his own individuality, his own opinions. Certainly you will find people with whom you simply cannot get along. To fly off the handle the moment you don't agree with someone, however, suggests an inability to get along with the majority of people who make up society. You qualify as a member of society only when you acknowledge the existence of people who hold opinions that differ from yours.

As a child, you were apt to put yourself in the center, letting emotion take the lead. But you'll soon be an adult, so I think it's time for you to begin acting and making decisions on the basis of reason.

This is not to say that reason is the supreme good. I am aware that too high a regard for it gives rise to imperfections of character that differ from those caused by too high a regard for feeling. Actually, the relation between emotion and reason becomes so complex that I prefer to postpone discussion of it till another time. For the moment, I'd merely like you to be aware of the importance of reason in dealing with your problem.

QUESTION:

I set goals and set up plans to accomplish them. But though in the beginning I can carry them out, I can't keep it up for long. How can I learn to stick to my plan?

ANSWER:

Perhaps you don't have enough will power. Someone can tell you to grit your teeth and stick at it, but it is impossible to build will power overnight.

You say you cannot stick to your plan. Part of your problem may be a matter of outlook. Even though you give up before reaching your objective, it is quite all right to set up a new plan and pursue it. Everyone experiences frustration on the way to a goal; in fact, getting frustrated is the natural result of trying to accomplish something. What is important is what you do *after* you feel frustrated. You dare not become discouraged and imagine it's no use trying. You must challenge the difficulty that tripped you up and muster fresh courage.

Once you can respond in that way, it is possible to feel things are going well for you — even if you think you can't stick to your plans or even if you think you lack will power. Though you give up before you reach your goal, so long as you continue to grapple with your problems you ought not think you have failed. That is the same as sticking to it.

People who can stick to their plan in this way do not lack will power just because they get frustrated. Rather, because they can get back up and try again without admitting defeat, we can say that they have developed a good deal of will power.

The key to the problem lies in persistence. If your plans fall through before you reach your goal, start over again. In the process of repetition, you will gradually improve. First you'll be able to stick to your program for a couple of days, then for a week or ten days, and finally for a month, until little by little you can keep at it until you attain your objective.

But you have to keep this in mind. Naturally, you cannot long pursue a goal that is unreasonable; and so it is necessary to give careful thought to devising your plans and setting your goals. Even the most brilliant strategy is meaningless if you cannot put it into practice. For example, unless one has the necessary funds, and unless the technology for executing brilliant concepts of construction exists, designs for a spectacular building will be of little use. The same is true of any scheme that cannot be carried out: it is meaningless.

Consequently, your aims and plans must be within your capability. They must be something you can realize with a bit of persistence. The desire to defy limits is praiseworthy, but sooner or later you'll run up against the wall by doing that. And besides, if the undertaking exceeds your capacity there is no reason to expect that you will be able to stick to it in the long run, even if you are able to make it for the first few days.

Enthusiasm runs high when setting up goals and planning ways to achieve them. But the psychology of that moment is, so to say, exceptional. That is not how you normally feel. Under the spell of excitement, you may try to do things that are somewhat beyond your power, things you would not usually try. You can imagine, then, what might happen were you to set up your project when you are in a state of excitement.

More often than not, it seems that those who cannot stick to things tend to concoct projects beyond their ability. When it comes to study, for example, such people — though they generally do little studying — tend to insist on ambitious goals once they make up their minds to start cracking their books. The point is that such plans fail practically one hundred percent of the time. The clever way to go about it is, first, to regard your decision to get something done *as a decision*, and second, to be sure to keep the actual project within your capabilities.

Then, if you execute the plan soundly, you may gradually shift to something slightly more demanding. If you approach the task in this way, you will not become unduly frustrated and your confidence will develop as you go along.

In any event, systematic planning is important to any venture. Don't let a few setbacks bother you but move ahead, mustering the courage to give it another try with a fresh plan of attack.

On Friendship

QUESTION:

I don't have any pals. When I see how my classmates chum around together, I can't help feeling envious. What can I do to get a close friend?

ANSWER:

It's miserable to be without a pal. Pals usually walk home from school together, discussing things like where they'll go during vacation. When you see them having such a good time, I can understand how you feel envious and anxious about being left out. But I do not think it necessary to get upset about it.

The reason is that many people have had the same problem. Even though they didn't have a real pal in junior high, they found a close friend when they moved on to high school and college, or when they went out into the world. Or, looking at it from the other direction, there are those who acquire good friends during junior high days but later on never find a true pal with whom they can share themselves.

Sometimes we find people who go hunting for friendship because they want to be on good terms with everyone. I do not approve of attempts to gain friends by misrepresenting oneself in order to get along with others. Although one can get friends this way, in the long run such friendships are only superficial; they cannot turn up a true pal. Worse, in the end the hunter after friends loses his individuality and no longer knows what friendship is. The result of catering to others, moreover, is not to gain respect but to be made fun of. Winning a friend in this way, even if it costs a lot of effort, results only in a shallow and remote relationship — a mere shadow of what true friendship means.

That is why it seems to me that there is some danger in

the idea of being in a hurry to find a real pal. If you go to pick up fruit from under a tree and do not watch your step, you can trip on the roots and end up with an unexpected injury. My point is that the most important thing for you at this moment is to cultivate your character so that you can become the sort of individual about whom others will say: "I'd like to be pals with him!"

You can cultivate yourself in your studies or in extra-curricular activities. Or you might do little things like cleaning up after classes or doing some small act of kindness for a classmate. If you apply yourself with all your might, you'll be developing your good points even though you may not be praised by anyone for your acts. In the process, you will develop in yourself an indefinable radiance and charm as a human being, and friends who are worthy of you will appear without your seeking them.

If one looks at people who have become close friends, generally speaking it seems that friendships develop between those with something in common. Fellowship begins between acquaintances on similar levels of development. As you mature, you will acquire friends appropriate to your level of growth. If you do not grow, the only people you can be pals with will be on a par with your maturity.

Your junior high days are vital for character development. During this time it is important that you have an outstanding pal. That is why if you are to acquire the highest level of friend, you will first of all have to become more mature yourself.

The famous French painter Pierre Bonnard (1867-1947) has said, "A person who cannot find a single true friend consoles himself by having many acquaintances." The Greek philosopher Aristotle (384-322 B.C.) wrote in his *Ethics:* "He has no friend who has many friends." One friend is fine. I think nothing surpasses the friendship that results from having a lifelong buddy who is just right for you.

Sunflowers always face the sun. When the sun moves, they follow its movement, changing their direction in response to the sun. The sun does not adjust itself to the sunflower but solemnly shines on, beaming alone. Still, the sunflower follows after it.

It makes no sense to feel envy when you see classmates who appear to be getting on well together. Shouldn't you at such times aim to be like the sun rather than the sunflower?

QUESTION:

A person who till recently has been a good friend suddenly became distant. I just can't seem to think of anything I have done to offend him.

ANSWER:

I think it is wonderful that when something goes wrong you immediately examine yourself for the cause. Surely you are a considerate person with good intentions.

That is why I think you should forge ahead confidently with your customary openness. When you examine yourself, change whatever you think needs changing. And if there isn't anything you think needs improving, then move on vigorously without fretting about things.

Adolescence is the time for rapid physical as well as spiritual growth. It is a time when your thinking changes easily. This also happens with regard to friendships.

You've been thinking you never had such a good friend. But before you know it, you'll be looking for a different kind of friend. It happens all the time. Moreover, since adolescence is a period when feelings waver furiously, there will be times when you break off friendships impulsively, merely because of a rumor, a misunderstanding, or for some trifle or another.

Adolescence is that sort of time. So even if you have a friend who becomes indifferent to you, you are not necessarily at fault, nor is he. Rather, I think this indicates that both of you are developing into adults.

Generally speaking, in most cases a friend is not someone you stick to forever. Both of you mature year by year. Your surroundings also steadily change. Thus it is natural that your friends will change as you change. Have you the same friends you had when you were a toddler? Or when you were in elementary school or when you started junior high?

The same situation will prevail as you continue maturing.

In the future you may often experience a similar cooling of friendship. You will be sad, you will be lonely; you will also cause someone else to be sad and lonely. But you must not conclude that friendship is therefore something that has no lasting value.

What is lasting about friendships during the teens is their

effect on both parties: they strengthen one's individuality. Your own personality gradually develops as you associate with many different kinds of friends. It seems wonderful to keep the same friends you had in childhood. But from the viewpoint of maturation, this could have a harmful influence on you.

Besides, out of the experience of repeatedly losing friends and gaining new ones you will eventually come to appreciate what it means to have a beautiful friendship bloom — one in which your hearts are truly bound together.

In that sense, it seems to me it is very important for you to experience feelings of sadness at this time in your life. How else can you learn the value of the beautiful friendship that will eventually bloom for you unless you have had such an experience a number of times, unless you have borne up under the ordeal? He who does not know the misery of losing a friend cannot know the warmth of real friendship. Now is the time of preparation when real friendship can be made into something with the highest value.

You also need another experience to prepare you for the future. If you have a friend who, just because he is your buddy, always tries to get you to go along with him and stifles you more and more, you should know what it means to try to escape that suffocation. Real buddies respect each other as people with identical liberties. They recognize one another's individual differences on the basis of mutual respect for each other as persons. Unbreakable associations are always nourished on the basis of these attitudes.

Friendship is certainly not where two people become one. Both parties remain separate individuals. But from their mutual contact with one another, each individual matures in such a way that one and one can equal three or even four.

QUESTION:

At times my opinions do not agree with those of my friends. As much as possible I'd like to get along with my classmates but I can't manage it.

ANSWER:

Sticking to your own opinions is important. It is also quite natural for junior high students to become aware of themselves as individuals. Thus a person who cannot state what is on his mind in a dignified manner is to be pitied. Nor is such a person acting like a junior high student. Nevertheless, I do not see you as one who constantly changes his mind and immediately adjusts to what his friends think, but as one who has quite a confident sense of independence.

Because man is a social animal, however, he must live in society. Thus definite rules naturally develop to guide social life. One such rule is give-and-take; when you assert your opinion on a certain point, then you must be ready to listen to what others have to say about it. Social life is possible as such rules are followed. That is the democratic way.

Moreover, no matter how outstanding a person may be, it is unthinkable that all his opinions are correct. The mere existence of opposing opinions means that a person can discover defects in his thought, areas where he was biased or self-complacent, and revise his thinking and make it more correct. In some cases one might actually become aware that his ideas were absolutely wrong.

I am quite sure that everyone has some opinion to which we should pay heed. As we talk over one another's ideas and ask others about their opinions, we will arrive at more effective conclusions. That is why we have such things as debates, discussions and the exchange of ideas.

That is also why, when a person becomes aware of flaws

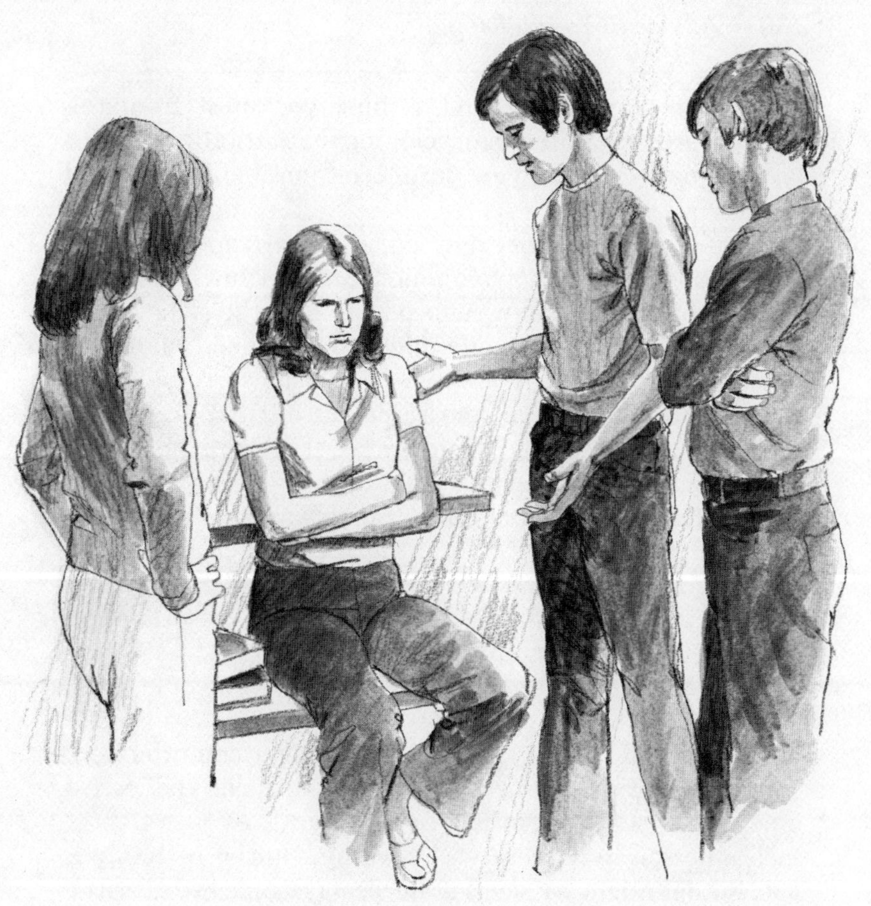

in his thinking, it is important that he correct his ideas immediately. The Chinese have the maxim, "The wise are quick to correct their errors." It is easy to misinterpret this expression to mean that even though a person may cut an admirable figure he lacks consistency and is quick to change his opinions. What the saying really means, however, is that the truly admirable individual is one who will adopt an opinion on the spot when he realizes its correctness.

Of course you cannot develop such a skill overnight. But

that is the very reason that I think you must from this moment set your mind on developing that attitude and thus lay the basis for growing into a responsible member of society.

From time to time one comes across people who constantly assert their own opinions and absolutely refuse to change their minds. But such people lack the skills to get along well in society and might indeed be called "emotional babies." If one is really a baby, he will be surrounded by adults who take care of him so he can get by. Naturally, such a person will not be tolerated if he acts that way among his fellow students in junior high.

Even if the "emotional baby" imagines himself independent, he really is not. He is merely self-centered and self-indulgent. In view of the fact that you say you try to get along with your classmates, it seems clear to me that you are not emotionally immature.

What then does it mean to get along with people? In a word, perhaps you might say it means to compromise willingly those points which ought to be compromised. Only those who follow such a standard can be called independent in the true sense of the word. At first glance, such a person may seem wishy-washy. But he certainly is not. Rather might we say that he displays some breadth as a human being.

No matter how correct you may think your opinions, nobody will listen to them if you are eager only to urge your *own* ideas. Which person do you suppose more capable of convincing others when it comes down to a really important matter, the one who always pushes through his own ideas or the one who generally listens carefully to what others think?

Only the person who tries to get along and who listens carefully to what other people have to say will be able to command attention when it is really vital to have others listen to one's ideas.

Actually it is difficult to decide what standard should guide us in deciding when we should persist in our opinions and when we should compromise. It is impossible to make a blanket statement covering every possibility because actually deciding how to make an infallible decision on this question is a task that faces us throughout life. But at the very least it is possible to say this much: always think how it would be if you stood in the other person's shoes.

Your life at this time is, one might say, in every respect a period of trial and error. At times you will quarrel when your opinions are flatly opposed. At other times you will probably yield too much and compromise your independence. But since each such experience is preparation for full adulthood, you must move ahead without fear of failure.

QUESTION:

A friend got mad at me when I told him about one of his faults. I thought I was doing him a favor. Shouldn't I have told him?

ANSWER:

Telling people their faults looks like it should be simple but it is terribly difficult. It's a pity your friend got mad at you. Personally, I feel like praising you for a courageous act.

One of our Tokugawa period Confucian scholars, Ekiken Kaibara (1630-1714), described true friendship as follows: "Close friends should tell each other their faults forthrightly. It sounds underhanded to criticize a friend behind his back. One ought to censure errors straight to a friend's face and praise his good points behind his back."

It is shameful for a person to refrain from telling a friend about his faults just because he's afraid the friend will get mad at him. Such an attitude shows that, though you may appear to be close friends, your friendship is actually superficial. The reason I say that is because such an attitude means the person in question is, in the end, interested only in indulging himself. I mean, he's only living for himself.

When your friend becomes aware of one of his faults, he might well wonder why you hadn't pointed it out to him — and doubtlessly he'll lose confidence in you when he realizes you didn't.

Even should a friend get angry when you point out a fault, if you try to keep from being upset he's certain to see the light. When he does, he'll surely be grateful to you. But even if he is not grateful, wouldn't it be enough if he mended his ways? I think that this is what friendship means.

Though people are clearly aware of shortcomings in

others, they frequently find it difficult to become aware of their own faults. That is why telling a friend about his defects when you notice them is important, particularly for cultivating friendship during your youth when both of you should be helping each other to strengthen your character.

The issue becomes clearer when we compare it to an operation. Although a person is in need of surgery, if a doctor says he'd rather not operate because it could cause the patient discomfort, the patient might temporarily rejoice. But in the long run the doctor is certainly not doing him much of a favor.

There is, however, another factor to consider. Sometimes, although we may think it a good idea to tell a friend of his faults, our telling him may not have positive results. Our motivation and objectives may be good, but because our method of communication is faulty, it frequently happens that a well-meant action spoils the friendship.

In the instance you have written about, for example, there may have been a better way to tell your friend about his fault. If one has his flaws pointed out before others, for example, it is only natural that he'll get angry. Or, if a person is told repeatedly about a shortcoming of which he is keenly aware, he might possibly think you're carping at him.

Furthermore, depending on how you phrase your criticism, there are times when it's best to come right to the point and call a spade a spade, just as there are times when it's best to be tactful and indirectly comment about the fault while you are praising something else in your friend.

Nobody really likes having his faults pointed out. People never find it irksome to be praised, even when they know it's only flattery, but it's hardly pleasant to be confronted with one's weaknesses, even if in jest. Well, we humans are, after all, quite self-centered.

And yet it's not quite so bad when our teachers or betters point out our shortcomings. But let an equal or an inferior point them out and we simply cannot take it without getting upset. Though down deep we may feel the criticism just, as you yourself have discovered, the fact is that a person resists advice and gets angry.

With all this in mind, you can see that telling a friend his faults is of itself praiseworthy, but you have to pay a good deal of attention to the *way* you tell him. You have to take into consideration such questions as: What'll he think if I say it this way? What's his mental attitude at the moment? How about the presence of others? What words should I choose? And then, once you've given some thought to such questions, it is necessary to endeavor to offer your advice in such a way that it will not produce a negative reaction but influence your friend to be willing to correct his weakness.

Finally, a fundamental point. When you caution your friend, be sure that there isn't the slightest hint of spitefulness, resentment or scorn in your heart. If there is, your caution will fall on deaf ears. This is to say, even a hint of such feelings is bound to crop up in the least little word you use, in your attitude, in your facial expression. When it does, it will strike a dissonant chord in your friend's heart. But if you have the best interests of your friend at heart, and if your criticism stems from the sincere hope that he will improve, then even if he gets momentarily upset you need not worry. For he will certainly think better of rejecting you after he has thought it over.

As you can see, then, correcting a friend is not simply a matter of thinking, "Well, I'll point out such-and-such a fault." You must rather be sure that you go about it with a heartfelt concern for your friend's growth as a human being.

QUESTION:

I have had a misunderstanding with my friend. I seem the sort of person people don't trust and, as misunderstandings increase, my classmates only say worse and worse things about me. It's disgusting to go through life like this.

ANSWER:

To begin with, you might consider whether you yourself are completely free of responsibility for these misunderstandings. I say that because in many cases you can avoid being misunderstood with just a little care, and because avoidance is often only a question of such trivial matters as how you put what you say or how you conduct yourself. In the event that you're always being misunderstood, that might mean you have a natural tendency to cause misunderstandings; you ought therefore examine yourself humbly and be on the lookout for such tendencies.

Quite apart from the cause, you should realize that misunderstandings and slander are practically universal aspects of human relationships. It might even be appropriate to say that there is no such thing as a person who has never been misunderstood. It's only a matter of degree. I'm sure that everyone has had a disagreeable experience or two along those lines. When you become an adult, in fact, misunderstandings become even more extreme.

That is why one naturally takes care to avoid giving people cause for misunderstandings. Still, it is not an overstatement to suggest that you should take it for granted that you will definitely suffer being misunderstood and that you will definitely be slandered. This may be somewhat of a bitter pill to take for somebody still in junior high, but that's how life is.

Shakespeare had Hamlet speak the following to Ophelia in *Hamlet* (III:i, 140): "Be thou (even if you are) as chaste

as ice, as pure as snow, thou shalt not escape calumny (slander)." Isn't that what I've just said? Well then, the problem remains: how can you live affirmatively within the framework of that reality?

In the first place, it is necessary for you to be completely convinced in your own mind that these misunderstandings and slanders are mistakes. You need this conviction in order to speak up and say that you are not really the sort of person others claim you are. Not speaking up is the same as admitting that what people are saying is true.

Even if you do not speak out, however, once misunderstandings arise others are not likely to find it easy to trust you. So you have to be cautious. You can't heal a cut by pulling off the scab; that merely delays the healing. And so even as you try to defend yourself, it is a fact of life that you might merely be opening yourself to further misunderstandings.

If you have said what you feel had to be said, then it is wise not to get too argumentative. It may well be a trial for you, but you must restrain yourself.

Then, in the second place, it is necessary for you to do everything you have to do as a junior high school student much more smartly than usual. Be a model for others, in studies or club activities or when it's your turn to clean up.

George Washington once said, "The best answer to slander or libel is to carry out your obligations in silence." It is important to demonstrate sincerity through acts rather than by mountains of words, for understandably what truly convinces people of your sincerity is visible evidence in the form of actual behavior.

Silently bearing the brunt of slander and pushing on without complaints may be bitter medicine for you to swallow. When you hear people slander you, you may feel that you cannot bear it. Others may regard you as a born loser and they may intensify their ridicule of you. I think, however, that the ability to stand up under such pressures is what ultimately determines a person's worth as a human being.

It is not possible to know the true greatness of our humanity when things are going well. It is only when things go against us that we discover our true worth as plain humans who can endure and overcome problems.

When you have managed that, most misunderstandings and slander will melt away. Not only that, I feel certain that what you once took to be a misunderstanding when people evaluated you will turn to respect. At that moment you will have achieved an important victory as a human being.

From ancient times, few have been as misunderstood as the great figures in history. Some have actually suffered constant misunderstanding for decades or even centuries after their death. But for a few, the tide has turned and today nobody is more respected or highly regarded than such a person.

This is a period of trial for you, so I implore you to persevere and thus transform that which harms into that which will heal.

QUESTION:

I have a girl friend. I've been told it's too early for somebody still in junior high, but do you think it's all right for me to go around with girls?

ANSWER:

Having friends of the opposite sex is, I suspect, something which interests almost everyone; you're not alone in having this problem.

Your interest is evidence that you are now beginning to shed your childhood and become an adult, and it bespeaks the fact that you have a wholesome mentality. As you know, some people readily think boy-girl relationships an indecent topic of conversation; I am of the opinion, however, that such thinking is in itself unwholesome.

Obviously, society is made up of only men and women. When a man and a woman join each other in love, they establish a genial family. This means that your very existence is a result of your parents' love. Consequently, the problem of boy-girl relationships is fundamentally noble and pure.

On the basis of this statement, it is my frank opinion that, even though we are talking about having friends of the opposite sex at the junior high level, it is definitely neither wrong nor something to be avoided.

This is not to say, however, that it is unconditionally all right for you to have "love affairs" like adults. It is indeed obvious that your relationships with the opposite sex be appropriate to your status as a junior high student. In consideration of the limitless potential you and others in your age group possess, and in order not only to avoid robbing the promise of that future but also to guarantee that the magnificent curtain hung now before the stage of your dream-filled adolescence will one day rise, I would like you to try your best to observe the following suggestions.

First of all, be sure that you formally introduce your girl friend to members of your family. And you also should be acquainted with the members of her family. Junior high students stand midway between adulthood and childhood. What this means is that you are not yet at the age where you can take responsibility for everything you do; in that you differ from adults. Some of you young people complain to your folks that, since you're anxious to do everything on your own, you don't want adults meddling so much in your affairs.

To be sure, there are instances where such a view is correct. In the final analysis, however, even as you complain about "meddling," the fact is that your parents end up being responsible for what you do.

Secondly, be sure you realize that whenever your grades drop and you develop a negative attitude toward life you thereby lose your right to have dates. The reason for this is that these are above all your basic responsibilities as a junior high student. You well might complain that adults can do what they want, but what would happen to them if they neglected their work and let their lives become chaotic? You have to keep in mind what is most important to you at this stage in your life, and only after you have properly discharged your obligations to school and family should you consider going out with girls.

Then, in the third place, I believe I would like to see all dating by junior high students carried out in broad daylight. It should be completely open and above board. Going to places which are inappropriate for a junior high student, dating in the evening and meeting each other on the sly will not only have a bad effect on your studies and your life at home, it will be condemned by those around

you. Under such circumstances, your relationship cannot survive.

These three points apply mainly to cases where the two of you are interested in being alone together. What I'd like to suggest (as one with more experience than you) is that you should preferably get together with members of the opposite sex in groups. I say this because junior high is the time when your interest in girls is just beginning to awaken, and you tend to lack perspective in evaluating the opposite sex. Thus it happens that one-to-one relationships at your age frequently end in failure.

What is necessary for you at this stage is rather to develop a proper appreciation of members of the opposite sex, including their strong and their weak points. If you unrealistically put girls on a pedestal or, at the other extreme, end up detesting them, you may interfere with the development of a wholesome attitude toward women. To guarantee a wholesome attitude, all I can say is that you must put the highest value on relationships that naturally occur in the classroom and during extracurricular activities. One-to-one relationships can wait.

That is why I wonder whether, in your case, it might be better not to limit yourself to one girl but to get to know as many girls as you can through group activities.

A girl friend! For those of you at puberty, the very word may make your heart skip a beat. That is perhaps a special privilege allowed only to those who are very young. I'd like you to try to avoid being merely enraptured by sweet words or sweet visions, however, but rather have the good sense to keep your eyes on your goals and to exercise wisdom in preparing to step into a fruitful adolescence.

QUESTION:

There are terrific examples of friendship in novels, but I figure I wouldn't mind being a loner if only I can be a solid and dependable person. Why is it important to have friends?

ANSWER:

Everyone is free to have, or not to have, friends, so it's impossible to say anyone *must* have them. Besides, making friends isn't all that simple, even if you set out to do it. In many cases, people only accidentally "fall into" friendship, and it would seem that close friendships occur spontaneously more often than any other way.

Well, then, I'll bet you are thinking that the only people who actually *seek* out friends are the weak or those who cannot stand to be alone. If so, then you're making a terrific mistake.

What I mean is this. True friendship is a matter of each party retaining his own sense of self, of learning together, of mutually respecting each other's personalities and strong points. The sort of relationship in which a fragile sapling is supported and braced by a prop, or the sort where you merely see eye to eye on some things or have the same hobbies, is a far cry from being true friendship. Real friendship is to stand together with both feet planted firmly on the ground and to be bound together by mutual trust. Consequently, only those who are strong and steady people can sustain a firm friendship.

Why, then, is it important to have friends? I conclude that we need them because nobody is perfect and because life's greatest task is to see how far we can improve ourselves as human beings. "If only I can be a solid . . . person," you say; but do you really think that you can tell all by yourself when you are a "solid and dependable person"?

One knows far less about himself than anything else in the whole world. Notice that not even the most famous physician can examine himself accurately. Similarly, when it comes right down to it, the truth is that even those with the best brains very often have absolutely no insight into themselves.

It may seem a trivial thing to be able to gain an accurate understanding of oneself. The truth is, it is extremely important for at least two reasons. First, only by understanding where you are at this point can you "lay the right tracks" for future growth; second, if you are not absolutely sure of your beginning point, your progress is likely to be unsteady and undependable. That's the sense in which give-and-take with friends is extremely important. Through such relationships you develop a sound understanding of your own strengths and weaknesses. In a word, you come to understand yourself better.

Equally important is the fact that you certainly cannot get by alone in our society. Particularly after you graduate from school and become a full-fledged member of society will you discover that you cannot get very far all by yourself. The individual's efforts are, of course, important. But out in the world you'll find that the extent to which you cooperate with and take joint action with others is far more significant than what you can do on your own.

Regardless of his abilities, the person who cannot work together with others will find it — to put the case in extreme terms — very nearly impossible to live in society.

School is both a place where one acquires information and an arena in which one perfects his character. One dominant aim of formal education, aside from the usual tasks of teaching and learning, is to create the basis for the individual's growth as a member of society through give-and-take relationships with friends. That is why it is perhaps no exaggeration to suggest that if you end up being a loner you've only gotten half an education.

In any event, if you look at the problem from this angle, I believe you can see how very vital it is for those of you at this stage in your maturation to acquire friends.

Well, then, what can one say about the terrific examples of friendship that turn up in literature and the like? It is certainly untrue that you cannot yourself foster such friendships short of discovering a very special friend. To paraphrase the old saying, you can tell a man by the company he keeps; that is why it is important to consider what sort of people you have as friends. Nevertheless, it is possible to consider the problem from the extreme viewpoint that, as long as you yourself are "solid," you might actually be able to change a friend who is potentially a bad influence.

That is to say that an ideally perfect friendship is by no means existing only in some far-off dream world. It is something you can cultivate right now among acquaintances you have at this moment. If the friend is as solid and dependable as you, there is no reason why you cannot develop between you the most perfect sort of friendship imaginable.

QUESTION:

In order to improve my class at school, I figure I can either become a leader or work behind the scenes. Which would you prefer?

ANSWER:

I deeply admire your desire to improve your entire class and not just yourself. It may seem to some that the class is none of your business, but it appears to me that you are concerned about others, and such a concern will actually contribute to your personal growth as a human being.

Self-centered people who escape into their own shells and imagine that as long as things go well for them they shouldn't waste their time doing anything for the group are most detestable. But worse, acting selfishly makes no contribution at all to one's growth as a human being.

The following story will illustrate my point.

Once long, long ago there was a man who took to the road with the idea that he'd like to observe conditions in Hell and Paradise before he died. Crossing fields and mountains, he ultimately arrived at the gates of Hell. When he entered he saw a table piled high with food; all the inhabitants of Hell had gathered round it. Looking closer at the scene, which at first glance seemed so cheerful, he found to his dismay that everyone was merely skin and bones. Because their chopsticks were longer than their arms, they could pick up the food but they could not transfer it to their mouths.

The traveller then visited Paradise. There, too, he found a table piled high with food, just as in Hell. And everyone was likewise gathered round it, eating with chopsticks longer than their arms. The people in Paradise, however, were overweight. He looked a bit more closely, wondering why this should be. He then discovered that the people in

Hell could not eat anything because each was interested in feeding himself, while the people in Paradise were interested in feeding their neighbors — and they, in turn, were fed by their neighbors.

This story came to my attention some time ago, but it seems to illustrate the point I wish to make. I think we can say that it teaches us not only how egoism ultimately destroys the self but also how a person who does things with other people in mind actually ends up contributing to himself as well.

But to return to your question. Should a person become a leader or work behind the scenes? It depends on a number of factors, including, for example, differences in personality and the circumstances that exist at the moment of your decision. Thus it seems impossible to make a sweeping conclusion. My personal opinion, for what it is worth, favors those who silently encourage others behind the scenes.

It's tough working behind the scenes. After all, a person doesn't stand out back there, and viewed from the outside people might consider his contribution trivial. But no leader can operate on stage without people working behind the scenes. Many are desirous of being in the limelight, a desire they can realize at any time if they have the ability; even if they don't desire it, if they are able they will naturally be nominated for the job.

In any event, we need both leaders and people willing to work behind the scenes. It is very much the same, to use a metaphor from nature, as a tree which needs both roots and blossoms. No blossom can bloom unless the tree has roots. Even with roots, unless the tree has blossoms it will produce no fruit. In a word, some people must serve as roots and some as blossoms.

The important thing to keep in mind is that, regardless of

the role one plays, everyone must have the same aim. In your case, it is to improve your class. When the aim is disregarded, those behind the scenes may come to feel dissatisfied with what they regard as unimportant roles; and when those in positions of leadership forget the sacrifices made by those supporting them behind the scenes, they may come to feel puffed up and self-satisfied.

People in positions of authority should especially be cautioned in this regard. They must be able to operate with the same mind as the others, even when they return to the rank and file and work behind the scenes. Those who from time to time assume positions of leadership generally detest returning to roles behind the scenes. Actually, such people ought never to have assumed positions of responsibility because they basically lack the qualification to become leaders.

It would be good for you to acknowledge from the outset the fact that people who take on leadership responsibilities often suffer being misunderstood even though they have no particular weak points. And such people will be envied by others, too. That is why leaders must be extremely cautious about making imprudent statements or taking imprudent actions. As you can imagine, the slightest provocation incurs antagonism, and even if one speaks the truth people will sometimes refuse to cooperate.

For that very reason, it's "curtains" if a leader entertains even the slightest notion that he deserves special rights that others do not possess. Such an attitude will definitely surface in one's words and attitudes, and that will inevitably result in the group's boycott. People of that sort are, in my viewpoint, most contemptible.

A person who has risen to a position of leadership will exemplify the democratic spirit and improve the group only if his attitude consistently shows that he relates to others as a coordinator, as an equal member of the same team, and as one who maintains pride in leadership and a strong sense of responsibility to the group.

QUESTION:

I've been given a nickname I don't like. Whenever I show I dislike it, the kids use it all the more. How can I get rid of this nickname?

ANSWER:

You've got quite a problem! Your classmates are probably calling you names not so much out of malice as out of amusement over your reactions: scowling at them, avoiding them, scolding them for all you're worth! That's why, it would seem, the more you let on your dislike the more you encourage them to continue — you go from bad to worse.

Here's what I recommend. How about gritting your teeth and accepting your nickname? Respond nonchalantly whenever they use it. You might imagine that you're simply not up to being nonchalant about it; that's when you'll have to stick to your guns. Since they're using the nickname to tease you, they'll certainly lose interest if they see you do not get upset.

Even so, in the beginning you're likely to get some negative reactions from them. But you're definitely not to let them upset you. Before long, I'm sure these people will tire of teasing you and stop using that nickname.

Another vital consideration — something universally valid — is for you to have something, some talent or strength of character, superior to those who tease you, something to make them say they are no match for you.

In most cases, a nickname is apparently not too complimentary. More often than not, a nickname reflects some physical or facial characteristic, or a person's manner of walking or talking; people attach such nicknames as "peewee" to teeny kids or "tubby" to chubby kids. And it amounts to a trial for the person so labelled because he's being made aware of a not-too-desirable characteristic he's already conscious of.

A person's value, however, is certainly not determined by the way he walks or by his physical characteristics. Being overweight or being short does not mean that an individual is necessarily inferior as a human being.

Such things do not determine a person's worth. For example, what determines whether a person is a superior junior high student is how earnestly he studies, how persistent he is in contributing to club activities and student government, as well as his contributions as a class leader and whether he is considerate of his friends, conducts himself properly at home, and the like.

Take a look at the feudal military leader, Toyotomi Hideyoshi (1536-98). This fellow rose from a menial orderly to a general who, in an era of destructive civil strife, unified the entire country. They say that because Hideyoshi had a somewhat ape-like face they nicknamed him "monkey." He absolutely refused to show his displeasure, however, and meekly accepted that contemptuous label, silently devoting himself to the tasks assigned him. By the time he became the leading military commander in all Japan, not one single person called him "monkey."

Imagine how irritated Hideyoshi must have been in the days people used this nickname. I imagine that, being human, there were times he felt he just couldn't stand it. But what would have happened to Japan had he spent all his time resisting his teasers or trying to dodge them because he hated being labelled a monkey? Perhaps these people would have doubled their efforts to poke fun at him, and he just might have spent the rest of his life as a "monkey" without ever having accomplished such ambitious undertakings.

Hideyoshi's greatness, we might say, lay in his ability to

tolerate being given a disagreeable nickname and to exert every ounce of energy to do what needed doing at the moment. Was it not just such doggedness, such determination — his endless ambition and persistence, his jaw set on showing people, "Just you wait!" — that made Hideyoshi the historical figure he turned out to be?

Now let's get back to you. If only you could turn into the sort of person recognized by all as "definitely terrific" or "simply the most," I do not doubt that your disagreeable nickname would disappear. Furthermore, I feel certain that, even should the name stick, during the time you convinced people of your qualities the nickname would be converted into a term charged with respect and friendliness.

There are various types of nicknames, you know. Those infused with friendly intimacy add a sense of closeness between buddies that cannot be achieved by using one's given name. Even teachers, it seems, are more likely to be given nicknames if they are popular with the kids.

But such names are not necessarily nice ones. One person has a face reminiscent of a hippopotamus so he's called "hippo." Another has a flat nose so he's called "flatface." If an outsider heard such names used, he'd think the person was being ridiculed. And yet the one so addressed might respond to such a name with perfect indifference.

When you look at it this way, it appears one can say that the problem is not whether you've been given a "good" or a "bad" nickname, but whether people use the nickname to tease you or to show their friendliness. Thus, in the final analysis, we come back to the problem of the individual himself. Perhaps the road to a solution lies in the direction indicated above: do not lose your self-confidence, do not feel crushed, but push ahead cheerfully and affirmatively to perfect yourself.